Gael Stack: A Survey 1974–1989

Essays by Rosellen Brown and Marti Mayo

Gael Stack

Sarah Campbell Blaffer Gallery
University of Houston
February 18–April 2, 1989

Dallas Museum of Art
May 7–June 25, 1989

This publication has been prepared in conjunction with the exhibition *Gael Stack: A Survey 1974–1989*, organized by Marti Mayo with Elizabeth Ward for the Sarah Campbell Blaffer Gallery, University of Houston, February 18–April 2, 1989.

The exhibition, publication and related events are supported by grants from the National Endowment for the Arts and the Texas Commission on the Arts. Additional support is provided by the Margaret Cullinan Wray Charitable Lead Annuity Trust and by Mr. and Mrs. Frank D. Dorr.

Partial operating support is provided to the Blaffer Gallery by the City of Houston through the Cultural Arts Council, the Blaffer Foundation and the University of Houston.

Library of Congress Catalog Card Number 88-064007

ISBN 0-941193-04-7

The Revisionist, 1987-88,
(detail)
Oil on canvas
60 x 76"
Private collection

Mr. and Mrs. E. Rudge Allen, Houston
William and Louise Anzalone, Round
  Top, Texas
Mr. and Mrs. A. L. Ballard, Houston
Derek Boshier and Patricia Gonzalez,
  Houston
Judy and Donald Bredenburgh, New York
George Bunker, Houston
Linda Cipriani and Gary Horning, Houston
Charlotte Cosgrove, Houston
Benjamin C. Crump, Houston
Alan and Martha Farrington, Houston
Joan H. Fleming, Houston
Ed Hill and Suzanne Bloom, Houston
Helen Elizabeth Hill Trust, Houston
Jinny and Harrison Itz, Houston
Lucas and Patricia C. Johnson, Houston
Mr. and Mrs. John Wilson Kelsey, Houston
Kathy and Karl Kilian, Houston
Dr. and Mrs. Vernon Knight, Houston
George Krause, Houston
Janie C. Lee, Houston
Sandra and Bubba Levy, Houston
Dr. and Mrs. Stuart Linde, Houston
Balene McCormick, Houston
Betty Moody and Bill Steffy, Houston
Mrs. Hugo V. Neuhaus, Jr., Houston
Nancy M. O'Boyle, Dallas
Mrs. Sue R. Pittman, Houston
Todd and Marianne Pomeroy, Dallas
Al Souza, San Diego
Gael Stack, Houston
Paul Stack, Austin
Timothy Stack, Houston
William Steen, Houston
William F. Stern, Houston
Mr. and Mrs. Alexander D. Stuart, Houston
Alicia Talley and Allan Smith, San Francisco
Paula Webb, Houston
Bob Wilson, Houston
Anonymous loans
Private collections

Dallas Museum of Art
The Gihon Foundation, Dallas
The Menil Collection, Houston
The Museum of Fine Arts, Houston
Solomon R. Guggenheim Museum,
  New York

David Beitzel Gallery, New York
Janie C. Lee Gallery, Houston and
  New York
Moody Gallery, Houston

Mayor Day & Caldwell, Houston
Progressive Corporation, Mayfield
  Heights, Ohio
The Prudential Insurance Company of
  America, New York
Rotan Mosle Inc., Division of Paine-
  Webber Group
Transco Energy Company Collection,
  Houston
Wilson Industries, Inc., Houston

Foreword and Acknowledgments

Since its inception in 1973, the Blaffer Gallery has been committed to presenting challenging exhibitions of contemporary art. It is in this spirit that the Gallery has organized *Gael Stack: A Survey 1974-1989*, the artist's first major museum exhibition.

It seems particularly appropriate to assess the development of Stack's mature work at the Blaffer Gallery. The years covered by the Blaffer survey, 1974 to 1989, coincide with the years Stack has been affiliated with the University of Houston. She was first hired as a part-time instructor by the Department of Art in 1974; she is now a full professor. Her work has been included in numerous group exhibitions at the Blaffer Gallery including Houston Area Exhibitions in 1974, 1975 and 1980, and Art Faculty Exhibitions in 1975, 1978, 1981, 1986 and 1989. However, despite Stack's frequent exposure in the Houston area, at the Blaffer and at numerous other venues, *Gael Stack: A Survey 1974-1989*, which includes thirty-seven paintings and forty-four works on paper, will give Houston audiences their first opportunity to view a large body of work created over a substantial period of time by this important artist.

An exhibition and publication of this scope would not have been possible without the large increases in funding from outside sources which the Gallery received in 1988. The Cultural Arts Council of Houston, in response to significant improvements in the quality of Gallery programming, awarded the Blaffer major increases in operating support; the Texas Commission on the Arts provided funding specifically for the Stack exhibition; and, for the first time in the Gallery's history, a grant from the National Endowment for the Arts was awarded for a Gallery-originated project. We are very grateful for generous additional support provided by the Margaret Cullinan Wray Charitable Lead Annuity Trust and Mr. and Mrs. Frank D. Dorr.

The organization of the exhibition and catalogue has required the full participation of the artist ever since the project was first conceived over three years ago. We have worked very closely with Stack every step of the way, and we greatly appreciate her cooperation, suggestions and assistance with all aspects of the project.

The Houston community has been especially enthusiastic in its support of the exhibition. We are grateful for both the community's continuing commitment to Gallery programming of this nature, and its increased support of Gallery publications. Recognition and thanks are also due to the members of our Advisory Board, many of whom are long-time supporters of Stack's work, for their generosity, hard work and dedication to the project.

A large number of individual lenders are participating in the Stack exhibition. Their cooperation has made the exhibition possible, and we are very grateful that they have agreed to live without their much-loved Gael Stack works for the duration of the exhibition.

We are so pleased that a portion of the exhibition will be traveling to the Dallas Museum of Art after its presentation at the Blaffer. We are grateful to Dr. Richard R. Brettell, Director, and Sue Graze, Curator of Contemporary Art, Dallas Museum of Art, for their enthusiasm and participation in this project. We are also indebted to the other museums, institutions, galleries and their staffs who assisted us with photography and in the research and location of works: Eileen Coffman, Manager, Visual Resources, Dallas Museum of Art; Gail Rose, Executive Director, The Gihon Foundation, Dallas; Diane Waldman, Director, and Laura Latman, Registrar's Assistant, Solomon R. Guggenheim Museum, New York; Walter Hopps, Director and Hilary Borow, Assistant to the Registrar, The Menil Collection, Houston; Dr. Peter C. Marzio, Director, Alison de Lima Greene, Associate Curator, Twentieth-Century Art, and Charles Carroll, Registrar, The Museum of Fine Arts, Houston. David Beitzel, David Beitzel Gallery, New York; Janie C. Lee, Margaret Griffin, Jan Burandt, Linn Swartz and Teddy Terhune, Janie C. Lee Gallery, Houston and New York; Betty Moody, and Lisa Barkley, Moody Gallery, Houston, have all provided invaluable assistance.

The University of Houston, University president Dr. Richard L. Van Horn and the University community have consistently demonstrated their commitment to the Blaffer. We extend a special thanks to George Bunker, former chairman of the Department of Art and long-time advocate of Stack's work, for his kind cooperation and goodwill. As a university museum, the Blaffer is actively involved in the education and training of art students through an internship program. Summer intern Dana Padgett, candidate for the master's degree in painting, conducted extensive research for the artist's exhibition history and bibliography. Interns for the fall semester, Monica Chau, post-baccalaureate student in photography, Suzanne Decker, candidate for the master's degree in painting and Kathryn Sherman, candidate for the bachelor's degree in art history, all contributed their hard work and dedication to various aspects of the exhibition and catalogue.

The Blaffer staff rose to the challenge of the exhibition with its usual professionalism and energy. Registrar Nancy Hixon coordinated the transport and photography of the works of art. Rena Minar, Curatorial Assistant for Education and Public Affairs, worked on related events and publicity with her usual intelligence and skill. Preparator Pat Burns and Assistant Preparator Steven Burtch installed the exhibition with great care and expertise. Administrator/Secretary Shiree Schade and her successor, ReShane Fowler, aided with countless details.

We are grateful to Elizabeth McMahon for her assistance with the Gallery's development program. We thank Richard Levy, catalogue editor, for his careful attention to detail. Robert Ziebell undertook the exacting task of photographing the majority of work for reproduction in this catalogue. Finally, we are grateful to Craig Minor, Cheryl Brzezinski and Susan Schroeder of Minor Design Group Inc. for their inspired design work, unending patience and cheerfulness in the face of impossible deadlines.

Marti Mayo
Director

Elizabeth Ward
Curatorial Assistant
for Exhibitions and Publications

Gael Stack

Marti Mayo

Gael Stack's art is an attempt to define emotions, to distill feeling into a form which conveys its meaning in an understandable fashion. Often characterized as "dark," "unintelligible," "difficult," and "inaccessible," her work is a conscious attempt to reveal content, not to conceal meaning; but to reveal, to "picture" elusive emotions and events, is difficult without resorting to sentimentality or illustration. Often seen as autobiographical, the work is specific to the artist's life only in her use of her own experiences as points of departure to achieve a more general definition of human reality. In a 1964 essay, "After Joyce," writer Donald Barthelme described the purpose of art: "The artist's effort, always and everywhere, is to attain a fresh mode of recognition. At the same time, he struggles to disembarrass himself of procedures which force him to say things that are either commonplace or false."[1] Barthelme's statement can serve as an apt summary of Stack's goals for her oeuvre.

Stack uses a variety of intellectual approaches and formal artistic devices to document experience and human responses to the events of existence. Always concerned with the variety of information that produces experience and the importance of simultaneous and chronological time, Stack's art touches the viewer with a sense of recognition, with reactions we all have in common. The artist connects with the viewer about threatening ideas in a nonthreatening way, reminding us of our common ground and startling us with our own recognition of the irony of the human condition.

Gael Stack was born in Chicago in 1941. As a child, she both drew and wrote. She says, "I was a quiet, nice child. I always wanted to be an expert, though. I kept silver notebooks for writing and drawing."[2] For many years her mother had a drawing in the family home that Stack had made as a child while watching the Army-McCarthy hearings on television. Her mother and several of her aunts were musicians; one aunt was an amateur artist who, Stack remembers, showed her how to create form with light and dark.

As a young woman Stack was not conscious of the possibilities open to her as a professional artist or writer. When she entered the University of Illinois in 1959, she began studying journalism because she enjoyed writing. Journalism, however, proved to be incompatible with her interests and, on the recommendation of a college advisor, she began taking courses in art.

Leaving school in 1963, her junior year, to marry a fellow art student, Stack concentrated on her role as wife and mother for the next five years. Two sons, Paul and Timothy, were born during the marriage and continued to live with their mother after her divorce in 1968. After brief sojourns in Los Angeles and Bloomington, Illinois, Stack returned to the University of Illinois, Champaign, where she completed her B.F.A. in 1970.

After receiving her M.F.A. from Southern Illinois University in 1972, Stack taught for one year at the University of Wisconsin in La Crosse, then moved to Houston the following fall.

When Stack returned to school in 1969, one of her first works of art was an abstract drawing concerning her feelings about marriage and divorce. The artist considers this work the beginning of her use of personal experience as a point of departure for her art. She has remained concerned with what is often termed "the ordinary"–her reaction to and analysis of the everyday events, emotions, and relationships which frame and define daily life.

Too often this emphasis has been seen as related to domestic concerns rather than as an introspective inquiry into experience, a recognition that daily life is important in establishing the tone of our existence. Perhaps because Stack is a woman, the work is too often placed in a context which is secondary to the heroic one assigned to artists whose stance may appear more exalted. Poet and writer Ursula K. LeGuin questions the basis for the common notion that women cannot create art of importance while maintaining an everyday existence. LeGuin says this common assumption is "a very noble and austere one, with religion at its foundation: it is the idea that the artist must sacrifice himself to his art.... His responsibility is to his work alone. This heroic stance has been taken as the norm–as natural to the artist..." and she suggests it has restricted the "hero's" ability to experience life at its fullest.[3]

By extension, we might assume that daily life is seen as the province of women, not men, and that art which addresses its meaning is not of the same stature as art that addresses war, politics or history. Of course, war, politics and history are the results of actions and emotions that assault us in daily life; the outer world simply mirrors our inner events. Flannery O'Connor, a writer Stack much admires, stated it clearly:

> *Art requires a delicate adjustment of the outer and inner worlds in such a way that, without changing their nature, they can be seen through each other. To know oneself...is also to know the world, and it is,...paradoxically, a form of exile from that world.*[4]

Gael Stack has used her art to distance herself from everyday life in order to comprehend herself and the world more clearly.

Stack's work had been seen in a number of regional and national group exhibitions before her arrival in Houston; her first one-person show took place in San Francisco in January of 1974. Her work at that time was very similar in intention and formal elements to her work of today. It has become more complex and skillful, of course, but her use of the vocabularies of color, line, composition and image to serve meaning has not altered. In a San Francisco newspaper review of this first solo exhibition, art critic Thomas Albright commented:

> *Her format is paper and her media include paint, pastel, crayon, pencil and collage. Her paintings–or drawings–revolve around one or two simple structural elements: a rectangular panel, a window of color, a human profile. These are drawn into complex webs of opaque color mixtures, dense pencil hatchings and calligraphic scrawls or lettering, all of which flow and leap across her surface with a fluid spontaneous zest and energy....[She] makes references to...Rothko, de Kooning and Motherwell...[as well as indicating] other symbolic reference points....Stack makes all these elements her own, however, producing an expression that is intimate, if cryptic, and that ultimately hangs together on the sheer force of a keen sensitivity for the visually appropriate.*[5]

By the time Stack began teaching part-time at the University of Houston in the spring of 1974, her work had been shown in five group exhibitions in Houston. Two faculty colleagues introduced her to Meredith Long, owner of Meredith Long & Company, and she was afforded her first one-person exhibition there in 1975. Stack would continue to show yearly at the gallery until 1981.

Reviews of the solo and group exhibitions of 1974 and 1975 character-ized the work as "darkly exuberant…emotional, intimate views into a rest-less conscience….derived from clever, unique sources."[6]

Throughout the 1970s, Stack continued to work and exhibit extensively. These exhibitions of works on paper were both critical and commercial suc-cesses. The artist did not begin to work on canvas until 1978, when, she says, the drawings had become so large they were simply impractical.

Untitled works from 1974, 1975 and 1976 and *Up Against the Wall*, 1976, are important examples of work from this period and illustrate the artist's command of the picture plane and absolute control of line and form. While they contain semi-recognizable, biomorphic shapes, the iconography is only one element in a rich vocabulary. Images and seemingly random marks are seen against muted grounds composed of arenas of complicated color–blue, gray, brown, yellow, turquoise and pink. Many of these works from the 1970s contain shorthand symbols, a reference system with which Stack became familar during her work as a secretary in Illinois. For exam-ple, one common reference is a hook-like mark which in shorthand means "no." Shorthand was a natural system of symbols for Stack, since each mark has meaning, yet the meaning is not readily decipherable to most of us.

While we are tempted, and sometimes seduced, by Stack's rich layering of images and ideas, to interpret, reinterpret and speculate endlessly on the ideology and iconography contained in the paintings, we often forget to consider the reason these works communicate with the viewer so effec-tively. It is a simple matter: Stack is a consummate master of her craft. "Content" in a work of art is produced by the artist's use of formal and visual elements–line, color, form and compositional elements–combined with an iconography which is overt or implied. Content is elusive; it is the part of a work which is difficult to verbalize, to designate exactly with words.

In *Up Against the Wall*, for example, Stack shows two opposing forms on a light ground. The painting conveys to the viewer a sense of opposition with gentle menace. The separation of the two forms, the marked and the marred ground and the use of line for emphasis are devices the artist uses to set up a sense of antithesis or argument. Yet, while the forms seem to threaten one another, they do not move close enough to engage in visual conflict. Danger and destruction are implied but are not imminent. *Untitled*, 1979, contains many smaller forms on a far more complex ground. Stack again uses the "hook" and other shorthand symbols, but the painting is far more sophisticated in its use of color and tonal value than we have seen to date. These elements are characteristic of all the work in her 1979 exhi-bition at Meredith Long & Company, her first of works on canvas. Although canvas will become as natural to her as paper had been previously, she will continue to work on both supports, exploring existence and its meaning in large- and small-scale paintings and drawings.

From the earliest painting in this exhibition to the most recent, it is evi-dent that Stack is an instinctive and sophisticated colorist; a deliberate result of the artist's way of working. She usually begins by laying in a col-ored ground with paint and then drawing over it, using marks, images and shapes that have multiple meanings for her. Her way of working is both additive and reductive, in that she alters the surface of the ground, adds and removes marks and shapes, adds new elements and takes out others, in an alternating and continuous process. She proceeds until the work's composition, tone, color and form communicate as she wishes. Form conveys content, but in Stack's work neither the content nor the formal elements which convey it are easily understood.

The complex formal elements of each work and the subtlety with which the artist employs line, hue and tone make the paintings and drawings very difficult to reproduce. Meaning in art is less accessible to the viewer in reproduction, but technical difficulties inherent in the printing process play a more significant role in the perception of certain works. With Stack, whose work relies so much on tonal value, it is especially hard to comprehend meaning when we are removed from the original.

The amorphous, organic forms with seemingly unreadable notations which characterized Stack's earlier work began to change in 1978 with the move to canvas as a support. In *Four Onas Dressed Up as Ghosts*, a 1976 work on paper, three figures float above a pastel ground. The drawing is a tribute to a disappearing tribe of Indians from the tip of South America. Moved by their plight, the artist has used them as the subject, but not necessarily the content, of this work. Onas, the artist says, dress up in pointed hats and pretend they are ghosts. This kind of valor, and the tribe's fondness for pretense in the face of certain extinction, is one aspect of the meaning of the drawing. Others, perhaps, are comments on the use of pretense as a defense and on a kind of bravado based on amusement and evasion.

Similarly, *Mildred Pierce*, 1978, one of the artist's first works on canvas, is a tribute to a character in a work of fiction who survived a number of troubles and losses. As Stack's early interest in writing suggests, language is an important source of inspiration, and she often uses words and phrases as explicit or implicit information in her art. In the late 1970s, her use of titles begins to be more specific, both in terms of the sources she employs in a particular work and as clues to content.

The sources of *Four Onas…*and *Mildred Pierce* are similar–each subject's life moved the artist, but the formal tools the artist uses to convey this empathy are quite different as is the content of each work. *Mildred Pierce* is less obviously figurative–two anthropomorphic forms "stand" in the canvas's extreme foreground, allowing them to relate directly and concretely to the viewer. The palette used is very somber, mournful. The shapes employed droop and bow as if they were weary. The meaning of the painting is, of course, complex; it describes the feelings of the fictional character, of all survivors, and defines for us something about relationships and their results.

Stack uses figures and images from diverse sources in her work during the 1970s, but after 1978, the figures begin to develop more specific symbolism, and her image vocabulary becomes more diverse. Overt references to books, words and exotic cultures replace personal references, at least on the surface. But as the artist allows her sources and use of symbols to become more evident, it does not necessarily follow that the content becomes less complicated or more readily decipherable. In fact, meaning, in Stack's later works, becomes more layered and less decodable.

After Gael Stack's first trip to Europe in the summer of 1980, her new references and symbols are combined with more complex compositions. The artist spent the summer in Italy studying Italian primitive painting. Her interest in Sienese painters, such as Duccio di Buoninsegna (1278-1319), and their use of abstract pattern and linear design were a considerable influence on her work. She was particularly interested in Duccio's ability to convey narrative using simultaneous action–several events taking place over time, but described in a single work.

Works such as *St. Clare Saving a Child Being Mauled by a Wolf, after Giovanni di Paolo* and *St. John in the Wilderness, after di Paolo (for Sandra)*, both from 1980, illustrate traditional themes in Christian art. These works are complicated and much more linear than the artist's work of the 1970s. A number of actions are taking place on the canvas, and we become aware of events and experiences being captured in both simultaneous and chronological time. As in Sienese painting, the action takes place in shallow space and is essentially frontal. Space in both Stack's work and Duccio's work is shallow space in which pattern and narrative are valued over the depiction of "real" depth. *St. Clare…*, actually based on a painting in The Museum of Fine Arts, Houston, depicts a number of diverse actions which exist in a more specific space than we have seen in the artist's previous work. This space is less amorphous–forms do not float in undefined relationships to one another; but in these two works from 1980, neither do forms exist in strictly defined space–the Renaissance's "window" on the world.

Gael Stack's work was included in *19 Artists–Emergent Americans: 1981 Exxon National Exhibition* at the Solomon R. Guggenheim Museum, marking her work's first New York exposure. The show, organized by freelance curator Peter Frank, was a turning point in the artist's career. She received favorable reviews in the national art media. Her subsequent inclusion in two group exhibitions at the Contemporary Arts Museum in Houston, *Four Painters*, 1981, and *Southern Fictions*, 1983, and *Fresh Paint: The Houston School* at The Museum of Fine Arts, Houston in 1984, cemented a growing national reputation.

Peter Schjedahl, a New York-based critic and poet, reviewing the Guggenheim exhibition for *The Village Voice*, summed up the work in a discussion which focused on the "temperament" of each artist. Schjedahl defined his use of temperament as having to do with the logic or particular reason for a particular person to create a particular work of art, saying: "Gael Stack has the most palpable temperament–laconic, perverse, and tough. Her scrubby, glowing, dun-colored paint fields, in which drift hectic, graffiti-like abstract notations, evoke a kind of voluptuous discomfort."[7] It is this sense of "voluptuous discomfort" that grows and deepens throughout the 1980s, as Stack continues to exact from herself ever more complicated visual devices to convey meaning.

In addition to figurative forms and an increasing use of the canvas as a support, the artist began, in 1980, to include more legible words for the first time since graduate school. Scrawled haphazardly across many of her works since 1980, these words serve to hint at meaning but never quite to define it. They, like her titles, are clues to meaning, not denotations of content.

In June of 1981, Stack's Meredith Long exhibition contained a number of works with grounds which resemble those of a blackboard. In Stack's home, a blackboard was kept by the telephone for messages, and the cumulative effect of the transient and disconnected messages interested her. *Secrets* and *Souvenir*, both 1980, are works that reflect this interest. The last blackboard painting, *Call Maureen*, was completed in 1982, when, the artist says, the blackboard looked so good, she declared it finished and retired it from service.

Patricia C. Johnson, Houston-based art critic, reviewed the 1981 exhibition: "Gael Stack's new work…is richer and more personal than ever…. There is the need to speak balanced by the fear of saying too much." In discussing the relationship between surrealist automatic writing and Stack's use of images, Johnson wrote, "It's the magic and metaphorical qualities of…[the image's] being which are explored and used as symbols of personal secrets."[8]

Secrets is the most literal and, perhaps, literary of the 1980 works. The painting has a blackboard-like ground which is set off by bands of gray containing random markings touching the edge of the canvas on both the right and left sides. The center section has a plus sign, the word "secrets" scrawled across it and strange anthropomorphic forms inhabit the lower edge of the canvas. Underneath the blackboard-like ground, the artist has written a number of secrets she was told by friends. Since, however, secrets aren't secrets if they are revealed, she has concealed them from the viewer by painting over them. Regardless of its "secrets" the painting has a resonant surface activated by Stack's marks. Its content is complicated and exists on several levels. In addition to concealing secrets so they will remain secret–an ironic play on words–this work suggests, as well, that our secrets, which "make us crazy," are never as frightening as we think and become less important when they are revealed. Sometimes, the artist seems to suggest, we need to free ourselves from our secrets.

Souvenir (The Anton Christian Painting), also from 1980, is related to *Secrets*, but makes use of a number of pictorial devices and images not evident in the work discussed above. It pictures a figure lying on a stage. The artist has created a shallow space on which the action can take place. The painting is named for an Austrian colleague of Stack's who was a visiting artist at the University of Houston, and Stack regards the painting as a "marker" for Christian's visit, a souvenir. The reclining figure is a reinterpretation of Henri Rousseau's (1844-1910) *Sleeping Gypsy*, but it is not a direct reference. Stack recreated a version of the figure she had seen in the drawing of a retarded person. The work contains a variety of other references, among them one to the work of Caspar David Friedrich (1774-1840), a German painter of mysterious, dramatic and romantic landscapes who often depicted the transience of human life against the endurance of nature.

Souvenir is an interesting example of Stack's uncanny ability to use artistic devices and unusual image combinations to convey multiple meanings to the viewer. For example, by placing the figure on a stage in the middle ground of the composition, she has indicated our distance from the action: this is not a picture in which an active voice is heard, but rather one in which we are viewing a remembered set of feelings about an event. Typical of Stack's work, *Souvenir* transcends the immediate event–the Christian visit–to become a metaphor for all remembered events. It is a discussion, if you will, about souvenirs and why they are meaningful, about transient relationships and events, about time and memory and dreams.

When discussing her work, Stack talks not in terms of form, color or light, but objects, associations and meanings. She is interested in words, stories and anecdotes, in implied messages rendered accessible through irony and humor. She intends her paintings to reach others the way a good story does, to illuminate with a flash of recognition those things we all have in common. Her work contains threads which attract us to explore feeling in a nonthreatening manner.

For example, *Up Against the Wall*, 1976, resulted from the artist seeing a large number of mole pelts mounted on the walls in a gallery at the Museum of Natural History in New York. References to crucifixion, vulnerability and helplessness, all threatening events or states of being, are pictured with humor and irony. The title contributes its own connotations. A recent drama review in *The New York Times* quotes playwright Wendy Wasserman: "Serious issues and serious people can be quite funny....I think that's quite important. The thing about comedy is that it avoids self-pity. It punctures self-obsession."[9]

Wasserman might as well be speaking of Stack, whose detached amusement makes her work approachable. In addition to the "blackboard" paintings, Stack's 1981 exhibition at Meredith Long & Company contained a drawing of a mummified cat, *Untitled (Mummified Cat)*, 1982. The image reflects the artist's amazement at having seen mummies of every conceivable kind in the British Museum in London.

Though these images are humorous and ironic, their meaning is more elusive than a simple, funny comment about mummified cats, Egyptians or the recent loss of a Stack family pet. The image becomes a symbol for a distillation of feelings about loss. Art critic Susan Freudenheim has written, quoting the artist: "Stack says she often uses a specific personal incident as a starting point for communicating larger ideas: 'I made a painting about my cat dying once; no one else should have to care about my cat dying– that's not the point. It was also about the impermanence of things, which I think everyone understands.'"[10]

The 1981 Meredith Long exhibition was rich in a number of ideas and images which would continue to appear in Stack's work through the early 1980s. The artist began to use certain images which would come to symbolize specific emotional states. An ever richer vocabulary of images from life and the art of the past enabled the artist to elicit a variety of responses.

If surrealism can be characterized as the bizzare juxtaposition of unrelated images to produce new meaning, then certainly Stack has used surrealist theory in her work. This juxtaposition of unrelated images allows the artist, in her words, to "make paintings which are about ideas from within and from without ourselves…to put odd things together to make a third thing." She assumes the viewer to be intelligent and interested, and combining images in new ways allows her to create a vehicle through which she can filter the information which defines experience. She believes that although feelings have names, they and their sources are really nonspecific. She says, "If you look at the feeling, all the way around it, then maybe you can capture it."

Untitled (Gael Stack at the Guggenheim), 1981, is a small drawing which contains a figure representing, at the same time, the artist and each of us who has faced a new situation. It speaks to our definition of ourselves and the sum of experience which conditions our reactions to events in our lives. This use of the figure to demystify emotion is common in Stack's work. It is about simultaneously stripping away and adding layers of meaning. It is at the same time specific and non-specific. As a result, it successfully resists decoding or rigorous analysis. Stack likes the words of Alice Neel: "For all I know, my human images originate in terror."[11]

After 1982, a change in the work again occurred, consolidating and refining the developments of the late 1970s and early 1980s, while at the same time introducing a number of new formal devices and refining the new vocabulary of images. Stack's 1983 exhibition at Janie C. Lee Gallery was comprised primarily of a series of paintings on grounds consisting of mainly red and orange hues. In the "orange" paintings, whose grounds were inspired by the dominant colors found in frescos at Pompeii, Stack is at her most reductive. She tried to remove all superfluous elements, concentrating only on the information necessary. The orange paintings are a rich combination of warm hues, interrupted by greens, yellows, browns and reds which activate the surface, controlling the movement of our eye across the painting and directing our attention to the iconography contained in the work.

The Disquieting Object, 1983, one of the most reductive of these works, depicts a reclining figure floating in very undefined space–something which hadn't occurred in the work for several years. The figure is taken from a representation of a person being compressed by a medieval torture machine–the opposite of being "stretched on the rack." The compression machine and the small figure in the painting symbolize circumstances from without which act on all of us, compressing our freedom to act.

Gael Stack's work from 1983 forward uses a new kind of iconography of the figure. More fully described, drawn in contour with the emphasis on gesture as a carrier of expression, these figures dominate the canvas in size and importance. Many of the new figures can, in fact, be characterized or classified by gesture, and we see several "types" which occur over and over in the work. They rest, they stoop, they crawl, they face the viewer, they walk away from the viewer, they sit, they stand. In each case, the figures represent specific events and universal states of feeling.

The artist uses a variety of sources for the figures. Some are inspired by photographs casually snapped by Stack herself. Such a figure is found in *The Goodbye*, 1983, one of the first in which a large figure dominates the composition. A stooping, sad posture is assumed by the figure, which turns away, gazing somewhere into the space below the canvas. Drawn beautifully–Stack's drawing is rarely remarked on, and she is a consummate draftsman–across the two panels of the diptych that comprise the painting, *The Goodbye* speaks powerfully about memory, separation and isolation.

Stack's next series of paintings is termed "lessons." She returned to darker grounds in these new works, some of which have the word "lesson" in the title. The most complicated of the artist's works to this time, they were shown in a group at Janie C. Lee Gallery in 1985, and are stunningly beautiful. The artist has said, "The lessons were things I learned about life and art." Suzanne Bloom and Ed Hill, reviewing the show for *Artforum* magazine, wrote: "For the most part, 'lessons' have been used as a code word for those tragicomic moments that comprise one's confrontation with the world. With disarming honesty, Stack implicates herself in the recurrent drama and folly of existence."[12]

In *Lesson 4 (for Al)*, 1985, the artist employs another figure, this one taken from the reproduction of a headless Greek statue. If *The Goodbye* is about loss, the "lessons" are about folly. On the canvas the words "you could be sick" are written, a reference to that terrible idea that we can be comforted in a current misfortune by contemplating a worse fate. In spite of these clues, the work, like all of Stack's oeuvre, resists direct analysis. It contains formal characteristics common to the artist's work in the 1980s. Stack has arranged the figure to right of center and balanced it with a vague image drawn in red. Not drawn in contour but rather described by a series of short lines which outline the form, the second figure is a "crawler," taken from a postcard reproduction of a folk-art image of a woman on her knees. It is more fugitive, less permanent in feeling than the major figure, but interacts with other images and markings on the canvas in mysterious and important ways. The artist's wealth of marks and images move and swirl around the canvas, intersecting and layering over and beneath one another. It is this uncanny ability of Stack's to scatter visual weight and density to just the right point that distinguishes these works and the ones that follow from their predecessors. Suzanne Bloom and Ed Hill commented:

> *Stack prompts…response by her careful management of spatial cues and the use of open line drawing in which figures and text are overlaid, interwoven, and at the same time articulated by distinct color separation…. A painting appears to be complete when a certain critical mass has been achieved, one capable of lending depth as well as opportunity to meaning.*[13]

Rose's Last Summer, 1985, is a painting whose title, like that of *Mildred Pierce*, is based on a mystery novel. The title of the painting also contains other, inescapable literary associations: "a rose is a rose is a rose," "a rose by any other name…," "the last rose of summer," etc. The canvas contains a large central figure flanked by two smaller ones. The central figure, a "walking away" image, represents the artist, the viewer, the artist's mother, our mothers, ourselves as mothers, all mothers. The multiple meanings that can be assigned to this representation are characteristic of all Stack's figures. Simultaneously stripping away and adding layers of meaning, it is, like her other work, at once specific and nonspecific. Again, the work resists strict decoding or traditional analysis.

The central figure in *Rose's Last Summer* has its back to us. The two smaller figures are taken from a work by Paul Gauguin (1843-1903), the woodcut, *Banana Carrier*, 1899. Each carries a burden. Gael Stack's use of irony, and even a touch of black humor, is often evident in her use of these symbolic figures and her use of language in titles. In this case, we cannot escape the title's implications. The "end of summer" is a powerful signifier with several contradictory connotations. It is a time of nostalgia, the end of a fruitful, productive time of year in nature, to be followed by hibernation and death. Conversely, it is a time of new beginnings: school opens, the weather becomes cooler, we are energized. We leave the lazy days and return to a more productive, benign existence. The year marches to its inevitable end.

Gael Stack has always used a variety of references or quotations from other sources which she transforms to serve her own intentions. Her subtle use of these sources is decidedly different from the methodology of artists who appropriate immediately recognizable images from art and culture to serve their ends. What we have come to call "appropriation" in art is far more direct and less surreal than Stack's idiosyncratic use of "found" images. For Stack, her sources are points of departure; for artists interested in appropriation, sources are ends in themselves and act as subject and content.

Charles Jencks, a British architecture critic, wrote in the essay, *What is Post-Modernism?*: "The Post-Modern Age is a time of incessant choosing. It's an era when no orthodoxy can be adopted without self-consciousness and irony, because all traditions seem to have some validity….Pluralism, the 'ism' of our time, is both the great problem and the great opportunity…."[14]

Jencks' description of the post-modernist "incessant choosing" only partly describes Stack's working methods. She also chooses which evidence of process to leave on the canvas as she works–which words, marks, and images to incorporate in a work of art to produce meaning. In *Rose's Last Summer*, Stack has used Gauguin's figures as a resonant source for the expressionist poses of the figures in her work, not as central subject matter or cultural comment. Similarly, in the earlier *Lesson 3 (for Janie)*, 1984, the artist used images from works by artists as diverse as Edgar Degas (1834-1917), Pablo Picasso (1881-1973) and R. B. Kitaj (b. 1932).

Rose's Last Summer, like *Souvenir*, is concerned with memory, remembered experience and their definition and meaning. Stack's references serve these larger explorations.

Gael Stack lived and worked in London during the spring semester of 1986, teaching in the University of Houston's London Program. During this time, she completed a number of very dense and complex works on paper. (Stack has always been able to work wherever she lived. Even during the late 1960s and early 1970s when she moved almost yearly, she was always able to paint. Perhaps her early reluctance to work on canvas resulted from the ease with which she could transport works on paper and the small amount of studio space such works required.) The London drawings were shown the following year at Janie C. Lee Gallery in Houston. *Untitled*, *Hedge* and *T(oa)d*, all from 1986, are covered with networks of lines, words, numbers and images which are so intertwined that they become the grounds of the works. In contrast to *Rose's Last Summer*, where the figures are dominant and exist on top of the ground, the London drawings allow the ground to become the work's most prominent element. This conflict between figure and ground is characteristic of Stack's work throughout the fifteen-year period covered by the exhibition. In one series or work, the ground will dominate and the artist will activate the surface in a nonhierarchical manner; in another, a form or figure emerges and dominates the composition.

Belayed, a 1987 work on canvas, allows a lone, central figure to dominate. A dark and moody work, *Belayed* speaks eloquently of solitude. The figure, which was taken from an image the artist found in a medieval woodcut, is drawn in contour and stands gracefully in classic contrapposto, all the weight on one foot, the figure throwing one hip higher than the other and bending the unweighted knee, arms held behind the back, head bowed. Stack is interested in medieval woodcuts because the technique demanded an exaggerated pose to produce a successful print. The word "belay" means to secure or make fast with a rope–in mountain climbing, one is often "belayed"–and there is a looping line around the figure's weight-bearing ankle. As does *The Disquieting Object*, *Belayed* implies a quiet tension and speaks of arbitrary decisions, forces outside our own control, a loss of ability to act.

Belayed and a group of other paintings from 1987 and 1988, form a new cycle or series of paintings by the artist, most of which are larger in scale than her previous works on canvas. Stack changed studios in the summer of 1987 for the first time in over ten years, and the new, larger space allowed the work to grow in scale. The 1987–88 paintings, an astonishing series of powerful works, were shown in New York at David Beitzel Gallery. *Belayed* is the most "empty" of these works, the one in which the figure most dominates the ground. Other works in this series abound with Stack's welter of references, cues and clues to meaning. *Mild Warnings*, 1987, contains the same figure as *Belayed*, but it is surrounded with notations, words, and numbers, as well as a variety of recognizable images taken from a number of sources. Jencks's theories help explain the success of these paintings.

> *The challenge for a Post-Modern Hamlet, confronted by an* embarras de richesses, *is to choose and combine traditions selectively, to select…those aspects from the past and present which appear most relevant to the job at hand. The resultant creation, if successful, will be a striking synthesis of traditions….*[15]

Flor, 1987, is a large diptych with a figure in the right panel which was inspired by a painting by Hieronymus Bosch (1480-1515). *Flor* contains a number of other references to art history as well as a variety of notations from other origins. It is a depiction of change or impermanence, and signifies leaving behind the familiar.

A compelling work, *Flor* is remarkable for its use of color and the artist's control of "critical mass" densities: she crowds images on the left panel and leaves the right relatively open or free of reference. Balanced in weight and tone, the painting forms a complementary unity in spite of the disparity between the two panels. The artist's skillful control of tonal values unites them and allows our eye to move smoothly across both panels while at the same time enabling us to understand that Stack is making a distinction between two sets of experiences. The use of the diptych form allows the artist to load the painting with ever more complicated layers of meaning. The St. Sebastian figure in the left panel contrasts with an unbound figure in the right. The right figure dominates the ground on which it is placed; the left is merged into a welter of words, lines and images. As French critic Gérard-Georges Lemaire commented in the catalogue that accompanied a group exhibition in Paris in which Stack's work was included, "Stack…fills the canvas with significant fragments that circulate and scatter…condense and scatter…. They are equally significant scrapes of experience. A disquiet and anguish which is without drama emerges."[16]

Like all of the artist's work, these two canvases are simultaneously specific and nonspecific. Their elusive nature allows each of us to approach them according to our own world view. Jencks writes about postmodernism: "Its best works are characteristically double-coded and ironic, making a feature of the wide choice, conflict and discontinuity of traditions, because this heterogeneity most clearly captures our pluralism."[17]

During the 1987-88 holiday season, Stack began work on three major canvases which contain images of infants. *Bill, The Christmas Picture* and *Untitled* are distillations of many ideas communicated to the viewer through the use of diverse associations. As is always the case with Stack's work, the "baby" paintings are characterized by their multiple meanings.

The image is a loaded one; babies have so many fortunate and unfortunate associations in today's culture. They are, as well, comments on the simultaneity of time: babies signify both our past and our future.

Ultimately, however, these works are about power and its signifiers. Stack became interested in the bizarre appearance of infants in Renaissance painting. She was fascinated by the depiction of children whose bodies possess adult characteristics. Artists of the Renaissance gave these icons of Christ and the saints power by depicting them with mature facial features and musculature. Stack did not, however, pursue her interest in such images of infants from a single set of sources. *Untitled* contains the drawn image of a turned and twisted infant whose form was adapted from a pre-Columbian figure of an old woman. The artist was attracted to the form because it represented her interest in time–several hundred years ago, an artisan had made the figure of an elderly person which had characteristics of an infant.

Bill is a very evocative painting; the large infant figure is at once tender and menacing, curiously balanced on the picture plane by the image of a toy. The toy has been reinterpreted by the artist from the 1930s comic strip, *Felix the Cat.* Stack reminds us here, again, of the mystery of time–a new person, an old toy.

These canvases, with their disturbing representations of infants, have a number of references outside art and art history. The artist began working on them after a visit from a nephew who had been named after her father–again, simultaneity of time. She was also influenced by a project undertaken with writer Olive Hershey. The Glassell School of The Museum of Fine Arts, Houston, undertook an exhibition of collaborations between artists and writers. Curated by Glassell exhibitions coordinator Janet Landay and writer Donald Barthelme, a number of artists and writers were paired and invited to create new work for the exhibition. The particulars of each collaboration were left up to the participants. Stack made a drawing; Hershey wrote a beautiful poem. Both works shared the title *Beloved,* a title taken from the name of a character in Toni Morrison's 1987 novel of the same name.

One theme of Morrison's novel is the need to destroy the past in order to confront the future. The character, Beloved, is the child of the novel's heroine and represents her past. Both the drawing and poem based on this theme are evocative pictures of sadness, loss and, at the same time, hope.

The Revisionist, 1987-88, is contemporary with the first of the infant paintings. The upper torso of a frightened or running man dominates the lower portion of the canvas. It is surrounded by a variety of marks and shapes remarkable for their grace and color. This especially haunting work is divided horizontally the way the diptychs are divided vertically. The lower portion is much warmer in tone than the upper; the lower is characterized by a richness of marks, the upper by their absence. The disparate halves of the painting are comments on our outer and inner worlds and our ability to run between them, to juggle them, to balance them. (The figure, in fact, balances a shape on its nose.) The painting is titled in acknowledgment of historians and art historians who constantly redefine and revise the past– a process which is as inevitable as history itself. It is also a reference to post-modern ideas and theories–revisionism, eclecticism, deconstruction and pluralism.

Works completed by the artist in 1988 and early 1989 continue to contain images of infants taken from a variety of sources, but the works have become more somber and the grounds less dense. *Untitled*, 1989, is much less specific in appearance than *Bill*; its contained information is more elusive and less available. Like *Flor*, it is a diptych with one side dominated by the ground and the other by the image.

The artist continues to use visual information in the same way today. Progressing from her early use of anthropomorphic forms to the human figure, from paper to canvas, from less to more sophisticated visual systems, she continues to refine her ability to control the information on the surface of the work and create an increasingly rich and complicated visual language.

Producing works which have been characterized as "a fresco whose subject is the erosion of time,"[19] in which "fantasies of expectation are forever being tested against the realities of experience, which confound desire as well as the rational ordering of our world,"[20] she continues to distill time, experience and feeling into works rich in reference and meaning. While she believes that "you never really have the whole picture," she continues to help us perceive parts of it, parts which are given to us with a singular honesty of purpose and with great skill.

NOTES

1 Donald Barthelme, "After Joyce," *Location*, no. 2, 1964, p. 17.

2 Unattributed quotations are from a series of interviews between the artist, the author and Elizabeth Ward, Houston, Fall and Winter, 1988-89.

3 LeGuin, Ursula K., "The Hand That Rocks the Cradle Writes the Book," *The New York Times*, Jan. 22, 1989, sec. 7, pp. 1, 35.

4 Flannery O'Connor, *Mystery and Manners*, ed. Sally and Robert Fitzgerald (New York: Farrar, Straus & Giroux, 1984), pp. 34-35.

5 Thomas Albright, "Unusual Art in S.F.," *San Francisco Chronicle*, Jan. 7, 1974, p. 41.

6 Charlotte Moser, "Three Current Shows Give a Good Sampling of Locally Produced Art," *Houston Chronicle*, Mar. 16, 1975, sec. "Zest," p. 38.

7 Peter Schjeldahl, "Stock Options," *The Village Voice*, Feb. 18-24, 1981, p. 73.

8 Patricia C. Johnson, "Viewer Gets Pleasure of Attempting to Unravel Mysteries of 'Witches'," *Houston Chronicle*, June 27, 1981, sec. 3, p. 5.

9 Mervin Rothstein, "After the Revolution, What?," *The New York Times*, Dec. 11, 1988, sec. 7, pp. 1, 28.

10 Susan Freudenheim, "Gael Stack: Narrator of Emotions," *Texas Homes*, vol. 8, no. 7, July 1984, p. 22.

11 Eleanor Munro, "Alice Neel," in *Originals: American Women Artists* (New York: Simon and Schuster, 1979), p. 120.

12 Suzanne Bloom and Ed Hill, "Reviews: Houston: Gael Stack," *Artforum*, vol. 24, no. 7, Mar. 1986, p. 125.

13 Ibid.

14 Charles Jencks, *What is Post-Modernism?* (New York: St. Martin's Press, 1986), p. 7.

15 Jencks, p. 7.

16 Gérard-Georges Lemaire, *Cinq x Cinq: Houston, Texas* (Paris: Galerie Dario Boccara, 1986), p. 29.

17 Jencks, p. 7.

18 Lemaire, p. 29.

19 Bloom, Hill, p. 125.

The Renaissance and the Radio
(A Writer Asks Five Questions of a Painter)

Rosellen Brown

I. Who Is It Accuses Us?

Who is it accuses us of safety,
as if the family were soldiers
instead of hostages,
as if the gardens were not mined
with explosive peonies,
as if the most common death
were not by household accident?
We have chosen the dangerous life.
Consider the pale necks of the children
under their colored head scarves,
the skin around the husbands' eyes, flayed
by guilt and promises.
You who risk no more than your own skins
I tell you household Gods
are jealous Gods.
They will cover your window sills
with the dust of sunsets;
they will poison your secret wells
with longing.

Linda Pastan[1]

The poet sounds defensive. Her question is rhetorical: she knows very well who accuses, and recognizes the frequency of the patronizing accusation, and she will not sit still for it. Her conviction ballasts her–that "domestic" life is not "mere," is not "minor," that art made of it is not art made by default, little knitted things, fragile bric-a brac, the decoration that adorns the parlor. She knows that the home front–oh, the belittling phrase, its contradictory spheres–reverberates with the sounds of the most intimate and devastating wars.

Unlike the poet, Gael Stack is not defensive, at least not superficially. She goes her own way and has always done so, downright incapable, even as a student, of "getting it right," doing it by the book, their way, in the prevailing style. (Thus, a little eerily, the drawings and paintings of her apprenticeship, although obviously less accomplished, don't look that different from those of her maturity, the way some few poets and singers are born with a "voice," that marker of individuality, that aural–or in this case visual–fingerprint intact.) Without the corrosions of high ambition or a tendency to describe her intentions grandiloquently or even abstractly, Stack has, on the surface, little reason to be bitter about attempts to deny the potency of her work. She has shown and sold a healthy proportion of it, and has been treated to respectful and highly enthusiastic criticism, both at home in Houston and on the fast track in New York, where five of her paintings were part of a Guggenheim show in 1981.

Still, still…to sit in Stack's house, which is textured and cluttered with evidence of the complex life of the woman-as-artist–oddments and artifacts: a frieze of masks staring down from the margin of wall and ceiling, a huge piece of antique furniture, all drawers, that has not succeeded in organizing her life into neat compartments, framed pictures drawn by her sons as small children, shelves full of the books of a serious reader, uncountable and eclectic volumes of art history, Bosch to Beuys, and occult phenomena, peculiarities like a monograph documenting the festively decorated trucks of Afghanistan, and in the studio, an ancient rug that is by now a palette in its own right to keep the paint off the half-decent floorboards–is to recognize the conflicting claims on the attention of a whole person. It is clear how unprotected this woman is from domestic complexity by anything more rigorously distancing, let alone excluding, than an answering machine. She doesn't have anyone to live out the role of wife and mother to herself or to her work. Without much complaint, then, rather with a wry fatalism, she (not so) simply has taken the life into the work, made the "interfering" claims the center, not the margins, so that they are no longer distractions but subject matter, and has made of her paintings an unpredictable, organic, dynamically changing, unashamedly personal album.

Still…to talk to Gael Stack about success and self-assertion–"It is the part about wealth and fame that's hard to get a handle on," she said in her statement for the *Fresh Paint* exhibition at The Museum of Fine Arts, Houston,[2] uncomfortable with the self-mythologizing she thinks endemic in the art world–is to confront her profound surprise, and a certain accompanying wariness, that her vision of what matters is taken as seriously as she intends it. (She ventures a slightly absurd view of herself arriving in Houston in the early seventies, two young sons and a fresh art degree in tow, doing the pick-up teaching jobs, two and three at a time, that pay painters badly, but happy to be able to support herself. One thinks of the isolation, austere and purifying, for which some well-known artists are famous–it is an image beside which Stack's life takes on the colors of a rich and slightly overgrown garden behind a makeshift wall penetrable in a dozen places.) "Outwardly what is simpler than to write books?" Virginia Woolf asked in *Professions for Women*. "Outwardly what obstacles are there for a woman rather than for a man? Inwardly I think the case is very different. She still has many ghosts to fight, many prejudices to overcome."[3]

Large emotions can be detonated by small things, Stack's album of images announces firmly but modestly, profound feeling encoded in the petty increments of daily life. Death, for example, whether of one's parents (*In Memory of My Mother and My Father,* 1979) or one's cat (*Helen's Dream*, 1978), is finality and loss, is irreversible, is inevitable; a painting is an open field, and on it, scale is not relative. Mourning or confusion or loneliness can fill whatever expanse of space the artist chooses to yield to it. *In Memory of My Mother and Father* is dedicated to her parents. Two bone-white stick figures (only shapely, complex sticks, these are) dominate the lower foreground; they seem to be doing a little dance of accommodation, facing each other but leaning back, each of them, away. A distinctly negative inclination. Between them, floating upwards, are shapes–x's, crosses, arrows, birdtracks, and all kinds of colors, subtle and raucous, that appear to be the consequences of their rapt entanglement. What does it say in the upper corner? Mother? Father? Rather? Bother? Matter? None of the

above? The force of the painting–considerable–is in the intricate reverber-
ations set off by the vivid dance, the ambivalence and inevitability of it,
and all the attendant life that lies behind and issues out of it: the family
dance. The attempt to look at the charged movement–it is both tense
and playful, simultaneously–and comprehend it.

II. And How?

Stack likes to gesture toward a blackboard that stands against a wall
of her studio–"That's the best of all this," she laughs, or words to that
effect: phone messages, hasty notebook sketches, an ambiguous object
that looks as if it deserves a patent, quotes, names of books to remember.
Like the passing instants in a Frank O'Hara or a Ted Berrigan poem, those
shopping lists and random journal jottings that committed the fleeting
moment to a curious posterity ("If I rest for a moment near The Equestrian
/pausing for a liver sausage sandwich in the Mayflower Shoppe,/that angel
seems to be leading the horse into Bergdorf's/and I am naked as a table
cloth, my nerves humming…")[4] How strange, how lucky for the (male)
poets, that lines like these have always been looked upon as fascinating
glimpses into the flow, like action paintings, never accused of being
"merely domestic."
But in fact Stack's paintings are worked at, revised, built up laboriously
to look unselfconscious. What feels like O'Hara is tinkered with like Yeats,
who understood the hard demands of art on unadorned biographical fact:
"…if it does not seem a moment's thought,/Our stitching and unstitching
has been naught."[5] Stack's painting is far more grounded in tradition than
it may seem; its resonance for the viewer is a function of the composition
of controlled fragments that mime arbitrariness and quick, casual notation.
Her drawn figures, for example, usually turned away, reticent or retreating,
catch us by surprise because in the midst of this contemporary welter they
are classical–Renaissance heads delicately rendered, bodies reminiscent of
Rembrandt sketches, survivors of a less confusing time (*Hôtel de l'ouest*,
1985; *Mild Warnings*, 1987; *Flor*, 1987). *Hôtel de l'ouest* shows a lovely nude
seated in a darkness illuminated by neon-like flashes of life and color; she
sits alone, though in a different plane and separated from her by a set of
lines like a limb or a street or a river stands an ambiguous figure, dressed,
almost childlike, hardly the object of erotic contemplation. The scenario
here is timeless, one suspects; the classical inclination of the nude's head
and body poignantly underscores the universality of the experience com-
memorated at the French hotel named for half the world.

III. What's This "About" About?

"About-ness." The question is always a challenging one for a writer (whose primary language is referential, who has a direct relation to subject matter and possibly to narrative): does a painter want to use the word "about"? A lot of artists, after all, blanch at the word "about" for its literary connotations, its apparent refusal to acknowledge that painting has its own language, non-literary. When they say "about," they use it this way: "Glasco's work since 1977 is about…tone, color, unification of the surface, pattern in the service of unity and tension and rhythm."[6]

But Stack uses the word "about" differently, uses it with relentless frequency, unhesitant and unapologetic. What she means by "about" is her version of the impetus behind a painting, the need that culminates in a canvas thick with clues, with stimuli in the act of transformation into responses, with oil paint equivalents for emotion: the narrative moves between shapes, colors and open space like the flying steel bearing in a pinball machine. She doesn't care whether *what goes in* is intelligible (vehemently: "This is not illustration"); the challenge for her is to traverse the long distance to the point where *what comes out* has meaning, carries weight, speaks to the viewer's own preoccupations. What she concentrates on is the transformation from raw psychological data to a visually and emotionally convincing whole.

Stack likes to say, and re-say, Eudora Welty's formula for art, that it moves from *scene* to *situation* to *implication*. (Miss Eudora's notations, like Stack's, are not mystique-making but, on the contrary, modest, close to home, in a "domestic" language of gossip, front-porch wisdom and the questioning of received truth, family intrigue, the small secret whose pain drills deep, the small satisfaction whose pride calls forth muted exaltation.)

What the paintings are "about," then, at their source, means everything and nothing: their *implication* is its own world. For means to this end, Stack will grab anything that tugs at her fancy: shells from Japanese painting, suggested before she found the "right" shapes in Hokusai by an old fascination with the Max Ernst portrait of Dominique de Menil, which seemed to Stack to symbolize an ineffable innocence; flowers from Japanese gardens that look like the kind of sponge-stenciling children with energetic art teachers are sometimes led to in school, only these erupt like stars out of the black background of a universe of night sky; Renaissance babies floating through amniotic space or lying clenched on invisible ground, intriguing to her because the babies in those Renaissance paintings have such powerful bodies, a contradiction Stack says she finds "creepy." The I Ching speaks about the "taming power of the small"–here they are, then, these muscular little bodies imported into her work to be grappled with as exercises in both psychology and anatomy, emotional obsession and technical challenge.

The paintings are the arena in which preoccupations are worked through; what is visible to us is the ring in which the battles are being fought, have been fought, present and past continuous. Words float out of Stack's radio, one kind of ephemeral reality, hung out to wave in classical space. All of it is happening at once, the impingements of commercials, music, news, into the texture of intimate event, the ultimates of motherhood, womanhood, work, the diversions of pleasure, the senses, the weather. *How,* she asks, *can any less be true?*

(It is fascinating and characteristic, incidentally, to see Stack try to produce a print: she ends up treating it like a canvas, adding, revising, building up, so that she is left with yet another painting–she laughs–thoroughly unreproducible, like one of Cage's prepared pianos, a good many unreplicable steps from basic black and white.)

Is this a strictly contemporary layering? Remember the chill of recognition, perfect for the sixties, Simon and Garfunkel's news broadcast rising ominously against the hushed and holy background of "Silent Night"? Has she cooked us a post-modernist stew? But this is fraught, struggling, vulnerable art. If it needs a label, let it be what the sociologist Todd Gitlin calls "hot post-modernism"; if miscellaneous and wide-ranging, still emotionally committed, not ironic, and not detached.[7]

Look, Stack says, Giotto's narratives move round the canvas, the wall, from *here* to *here* to *here*–time viewed simultaneously, from now to then to then, apprehended all together, in an innocent age before successive events demanded different perspectives, separate paintings. Stack points her way around one of her own works: "See, all this isn't happening at once. But here it is, you start here," and we move clockwise. (Think about the word "clock/wise," the movement through time around the canvas.)

And then there is the layering, the way Stack lays down notation, word or shape, and over-paints, punishes the canvas to age it, then like an impassioned animal hiding bones in the yard (either to be gnawed on later or to commemorate a finished meal) covers it over, lets it lie, complex as archaeological time. She wants it to look old, used, worn and wearied. A palimpsest. Thus there is movement across the canvas, and movement down into it. A kind of cubist view of space and time, she says. Without being a cubist. Ditto surrealist. The Renaissance and the radio, repose and distraction, space and sound: the particular become–not universal so much as–available. *Her* emotional business transmogrified inch by inch, color by color, into *our* business. Emotion transferable to strangers.

Paradox: initially unlikely, ultimately sensible, perhaps even predictable, and the sign that Stack is no egotist, looking for mirrors of her own mind: as a reader she much prefers novels to poetry. Yet her work has been called–is like–poetry in its severe compression, its layers of simultaneous time and space, its emotional allusiveness. These solid circumstances that demand to be painted have melted, hung for a while wet and unformed on the canvas, then solidified again, this time as metaphor. Poetry is similarly dense; therefore she doesn't need it, she can do that herself. Novels, though, open out, are not distilled but, on the contrary, are expansive. And everything doesn't happen at once. A little breathing room.

IV. What Is the Lover Doing in the Garden?

One of those babies seems to be lying, chalked in, across the universe. "But if I don't grasp–don't see–" The painting, she insists, is "about" an obsessive question, in this case the toothache pain of guilty motherhood, all "what if" and "why didn't" and "if only." Her look could be withering if she let it. She picks up the Hokusai, a man (?) in a kimono standing in a garden, and administers an unforgettable lesson. It is called "Lover in the Snow." "This is a very mysterious painting," she says, and these are the questions she forces me to ask: What, in fact, do I know about this situation? Who is this man? What has happened? Is he coming to an assignation in the garden? Leaving? (There is no snow on his shoulders. Does that mean he has just come outdoors?) Is this tragic? Happy? So we read out of the carefully arranged hints–the angle of the lover's head, the conventions of position as (little as) we know them, and the feel of the whole–whether this has been a good day for the lover. (It has not, I think: isn't there a melancholy tinge to the mystery?) But she is certainly right: the familiar careful rendering of costume and stylized scene leads straight past situation to implication. The fact that it is "representational" guarantees nothing about its narrative intelligibility, nothing at all. This situation is no garden gate, open and shut.

V. What Did You Say?

A reviewer, speaking of Matisse's cutouts, said that his was an art "with no room for guilt or for drama or for pain."[8] Stack's, on the other hand, is about all those things, but with profound reticence. It doesn't much value disclosure, though it certainly wants to stir things up. If there are stories here they are whispered stories. The words that come to mind, in the face of these vaporizing half-secrets, these illegible contextless graffiti and incomplete assertions, are *wished, remembered, buried, forgotten, unearthed, unarticulated, unutterable, confided, accused, accusing, confronted, denied, withdrawn, retreating, broached, cancelled, proposed, eradicated. Dreamed.* Not *silent* but *unheard.* Behind the silence a constant chatter of fact, gossip, circumstance, shame, unspoken desire, loss. The poet's words–longing, guilt and promises. The catalogue for the 1981 Guggenheim exhibition may best have caught the contradictory feel of the tentative drama, the unhistrionic testimony of half-erased detail: "they seem to be telling us, indirectly but urgently, that *something happened.*"[9] It is profoundly a woman's art, I will assert, and take my chances with some critics, that uses intimate reference with such age-old modesty and so little concern for imposing it on others, except as a pretext to go and find our own emotion and haul it to the surface like a brimming bucket up from a well.

Notes

1. Linda Pastan, "Who Is It Accuses Us?" in *Waiting for My Life* (New York: W. W. Norton & Co., 1981), p. 34.

2. Barbara Rose and Susie Kalil, *Fresh Paint: The Houston School* (Austin: Texas Monthly Press; The Museum of Fine Arts, Houston, 1985), p. 170.

3. Virginia Woolf, "Professions for Women," in *The Death of the Moth and Other Essays* (London: Hogarth Press, 1942), p. 153.

4. Frank O'Hara, "Music," in *The Selected Poems of Frank O'Hara*, ed. Donald Allen (New York: Vintage Books, 1974), p. 91.

5. William Butler Yeats, "Adam's Curse," in *The Collected Poems of W. B. Yeats* (New York: Macmillan Publishing Co., 1956), p. 78.

6. Marti Mayo, *Joseph Glasco 1948-1986.* (Houston: Contemporary Arts Museum, 1986), p. 17.

7. Todd Gitlin, in a talk delivered at *Tikkun* magazine's conference, "Reconstituting the Progressive Tradition of American Jewish Intellectuals," New York, December 20, 1988.

8. John Golding, "The Golden Age," *The New York Review of Books*, vol. 32, no. 1 (Jan. 31, 1985), p. 3.

9. Peter Frank, *19 Artists–Emergent Americans: 1981 Exxon National Exhibition* (New York: Solomon R. Guggenheim Museum, 1981), p. 76.

Catalogue of the Exhibition

Dimensions are given in inches, height preceding width. For works on paper, dimensions indicate the image size rather than the sheet size when these differ.

Untitled, 1974
Mixed media on paper
21¾ x 28"
Collection William and Louise Anzalone, Round Top, Texas

Untitled, 1975
Mixed media on paper
21¾ x 27¾"
Collection Timothy Stack, Houston

Four Onas Dressed Up as Ghosts, 1976
Mixed media on paper
28 x 38"
Collection Mr. and Mrs. John Wilson Kelsey, Houston

Untitled, 1976
Mixed media on paper
21¾ x 27¾"
Collection George Bunker, Houston

Untitled, 1976
Mixed media on paper
10¼ x 13¼"
Collection George Krause, Houston

Up Against the Wall, 1976
Chalk, pencil and Cray-pas on paper
23 x 29"
Collection Solomon R. Guggenheim Museum, New York
Exxon Corporation Purchase Award, 1981

Untitled, 1977
Mixed media on paper
27¾ x 37⅞"
Collection Mr. and Mrs. A. L. Ballard, Houston

Untitled, 1977
Mixed media on paper
27¾ x 22"
Collection Charlotte Cosgrove, Houston

Helen's Dream, 1978
Pastel, graphite and oil on paper
27¾ x 37½"
Collection Balene McCormick, Houston

Mildred Pierce, 1978
Oil on canvas
56 x 42"
Private collection

Untitled, 1978
Mixed media on paper
10¼ x 13¼"
Collection Janie C. Lee, Houston

Untitled (Birthday Drawing), 1978
Mixed media on paper
20⅞ x 27"
Collection Todd and Marianne Pomeroy, Dallas

Untitled, 1979
Oil on canvas
40 x 52"
Collection George Bunker, Houston

Central Adjustment Bureau, 1980
Mixed media on paper
30 x 40"
Collection The Gihon Foundation, Dallas

St. Clare Saving a Child Being Mauled by a Wolf, after Giovanni di Paolo, 1980
Oil on canvas
40 x 52"
Collection Bob Wilson, Houston

St. John in the Wilderness, after di Paolo (for Sandra), 1980
Oil on canvas
40 x 52"
Collection Sandra and Bubba Levy, Houston

Secrets, 1980
Oil on canvas
40 x 52"
Collection Ed Hill and Suzanne Bloom, Houston

Souvenir (The Anton Christian Painting), 1980
Oil on canvas
30 x 40"
Collection Wilson Industries, Inc., Houston

Untitled, 1981
Mixed media on canvas
30 x 40"
Collection Joan H. Fleming, Houston

Untitled, 1981
Mixed media on paper
11¼ x 14"
Collection Jinny and Harrison Itz, Houston

Untitled, 1981
Mixed media on paper
11½ x 14½"
Collection Lucas and Patricia C. Johnson,
Houston

Untitled (for Ensor), 1981
Mixed media on canvas
40 x 30"
Collection Benjamin C. Crump, Houston

Untitled (Gael Stack at the Guggenheim),
1981
Oil and graphite on paper
10¼ x 13"
Anonymous loan

Call Maureen, 1982
Oil on canvas
36 x 48"
Collection Betty Moody and Bill Steffy,
Houston

Homelife, 1982
Oil on canvas
40 x 52"
Collection The Museum of Fine Arts,
Houston
Museum purchase with funds provided
by the National Endowment for the Arts
and Mrs. William H. Lane

Self-Portrait with Adolescent Son, 1982
Oil on paper
10½ x 13½"
Collection Sandra and Bubba Levy,
Houston

The Suspect Person, 1982
Oil on paper
11⅝ x 14⅝"
Collection Transco Energy Company,
Houston

Untitled, 1982
Mixed media on paper
11¼ x 14"
Collection Jinny and Harrison Itz, Houston

Untitled, 1982
Mixed media on paper
12¼ x 9½"
Collection Mrs. Sue R. Pittman, Houston

Untitled, 1982
Mixed media on paper
10¾ x 14"
Collection Paula Webb, Houston

Untitled (for Derek and for Patricia), 1982
Mixed media on paper
Two panels, each 2¼ x 1⅝"
Collection Derek Boshier and Patricia
Gonzalez, Houston

Untitled (for Paul), 1982
Oil and graphite on paper
9⅞ x 12⅝"
Collection Sandra and Bubba Levy,
Houston

Untitled (Mummified Cat), 1982
Mixed media on paper
9½ x 12½"
Collection George Bunker, Houston

Adios, 1983
Oil on paper
10 x 13"
Collection Balene McCormick, Houston

The Correspondence, 1983
Oil on canvas
48 x 58½"
Courtesy Janie C. Lee Gallery, Houston
and New York, and Moody Gallery,
Houston

The Disquieting Object, 1983
Oil on canvas
38¼ x 50¼"
Courtesy Janie C. Lee Gallery, Houston
and New York, and Moody Gallery,
Houston

For Miss Brave America, 1983
Mixed media on paper
9⅞ x 12⅞"
Collection Todd and Marianne Pomeroy,
Dallas

The Goodbye, 1983
Oil on canvas
Two panels, each 52¼ x 40¼"
Collection Mayor Day & Caldwell, Houston

Luck, 1983
Oil and pencil on canvas
41¾ x 53½"
Collection Alicia Talley and Allan Smith,
San Francisco

A Slight Ache, 1983
Oil and pencil on canvas
59¾ x 47½"
Collection Rotan Mosle Inc., Division of
Paine-Webber Group

Untitled, 1983
Mixed media on paper
9¾ x 12¾"
Collection Alan and Martha Farrington,
Houston

Untitled, 1983
Oil and pencil on paper
4½ x 3½"
Collection Kathy and Karl Kilian, Houston

Untitled, 1983
Oil and pencil on paper
4¾ x 3½"
Private collection

Untitled, 1983
Oil and pencil on paper
4¼ x 3⅛"
Collection Paul Stack, Austin

Lesson 3 (for Janie), 1984
Oil on canvas
50 x 42"
Collection Judy and Donald Bredenburgh,
New York

Untitled, 1984
Oil on canvas
47⅞ x 59⅝"
Collection The Museum of Fine Arts,
Houston
Museum purchase with funds provided
by Texas Eastern Corporation

Untitled, 1984
Oil and mixed media on canvas
50 x 38¼"
Collection Mrs. Hugo V. Neuhaus, Jr.,
Houston

Hôtel de l'ouest, 1985
Oil on canvas
60 x 76"
Courtesy David Beitzel Gallery, New York,
and Moody Gallery, Houston

Lesson 4 (for Al), 1985
Oil on canvas
47¾ x 60"
Collection Al Souza, San Diego

The Last Lesson, 1985
Oil on canvas
48 x 65½"
Courtesy Janie C. Lee Gallery, Houston
and New York, and Moody Gallery,
Houston

Rose's Last Summer, 1985
Oil on canvas
62¼ x 48¹/₁₆"
Collection Dallas Museum of Art

Untitled, 1985
Oil on canvas
52 x 40"
Courtesy Janie C. Lee Gallery, Houston
and New York, and Moody Gallery,
Houston

Untitled, 1985
Oil on canvas
48 x 60"
Courtesy Janie C. Lee Gallery, Houston
and New York, and Moody Gallery,
Houston

Untitled, 1985
Mixed media on paper
5½ x 3½"
Collection William Steen, Houston

Untitled, 1985
Oil and pencil on paper
3¼ x 2¼"
Collection Mr. and Mrs. Alexander D.
Stuart, Houston

Untitled (for Tim), 1985
Oil on paper
27 x 20¾"
Collection William F. Stern, Houston

A Girl Still, 1986
Oil paint and oil stick on paper
30 x 40"
Courtesy Janie C. Lee Gallery, Houston
and New York

Hackney, 1986
Mixed media on paper
27 x 44"
Collection Helen Elizabeth Hill Trust,
Houston

Hedge, 1986
Oil on paper
40 x 30"
Collection Dr. and Mrs. Stuart Linde,
Houston

T(oa)d, 1986
Mixed media on paper
21 x 27"
Courtesy David Beitzel Gallery, New York

Untitled, 1986
Mixed media on paper
13 x 9"
Collection Mr. and Mrs. E. Rudge Allen,
Houston

Untitled, 1986
Mixed media on paper
21¼ x 27½"
Private collection, Texas

Untitled (Audit), 1986
Oil on canvas
48 x 39"
Courtesy David Beitzel Gallery, New York,
and Moody Gallery, Houston

Belayed, 1987
Oil on canvas
60 x 48"
Courtesy David Beitzel Gallery, New York,
and Moody Gallery, Houston

Beloved/Boo, Baby, 1987
Mixed media on paper
28 x 37⅞"
Collection Balene McCormick, Houston

Flor, 1987
Oil on canvas
Two panels, each 60 x 48"
Collection Balene McCormick, Houston

Lemon Heart, 1987
Oil on canvas
48 x 60"
Private collection, New York

Mild Warnings, 1987
Oil on canvas
77 x 48"
Collection Progressive Corporation,
Mayfield Heights, Ohio

Other Graces, 1987
Oil on canvas
65¾ x 48"
Courtesy David Beitzel Gallery, New York,
and Moody Gallery, Houston

Ugly Patsy, 1987
Oil on paper
23 x 29"
Collection Nancy M. O'Boyle, Dallas

Untitled, 1987
Mixed media on paper
12½ x 14½"
Anonymous loan

Untitled, 1987
Mixed media on paper
27⅞ x 20"
Courtesy Janie C. Lee Gallery, Houston
and New York

Untitled, 1987
Mixed media on paper
21 x 27"
Collection The Prudential Insurance
Company of America, New York

Untitled (The Indian), 1987
Oil on canvas
60 x 48"
Courtesy David Beitzel Gallery, New York,
and Moody Gallery, Houston

Christmas Picture, 1987-88
Oil on canvas
64 x 84"
Courtesy David Beitzel Gallery, New York,
and Moody Gallery, Houston

The Revisionist, 1987-88
Oil on canvas
60 x 76"
Collection Linda Cipriani and Gary
Horning, Houston

Untitled, 1987-88
Oil on canvas
60 x 76"
Courtesy David Beitzel Gallery, New York,
and Moody Gallery, Houston

Bill, 1988
Oil on canvas
64 x 84"
Courtesy David Beitzel Gallery, New York,
and Moody Gallery, Houston

Untitled, 1988
Oil on canvas
66 x 48"
The Menil Collection, Houston

Untitled, 1989
Mixed media on lithograph
29⅞ x 40"
Courtesy the artist and Houston Fine
Art Press

Untitled, 1989
Oil on canvas
Two panels, each 60 x 48"
Courtesy Janie C. Lee Gallery, Houston
and New York, and Moody Gallery,
Houston

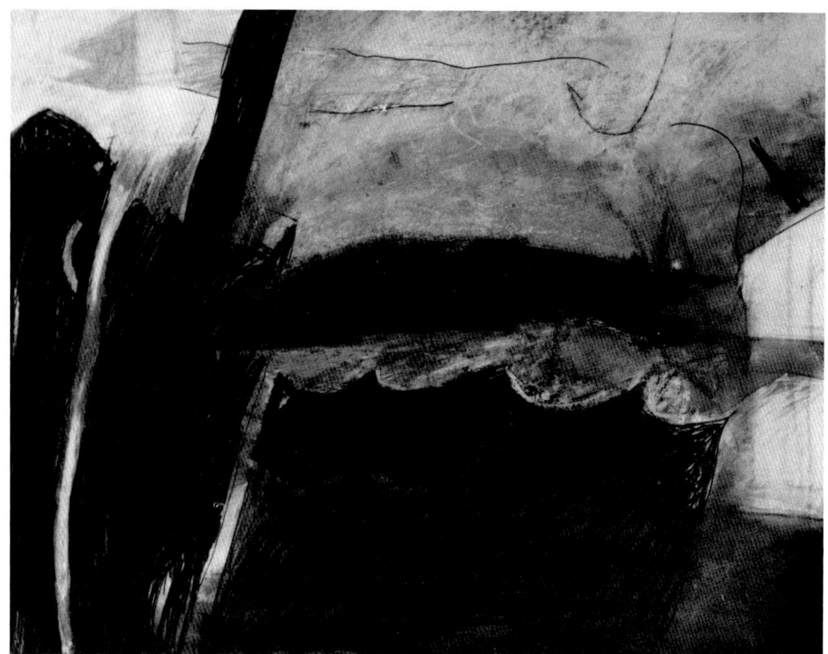

Untitled, 1974
Mixed media on paper
21¾ x 28"
Collection William and Louise Anzalone,
Round Top, Texas

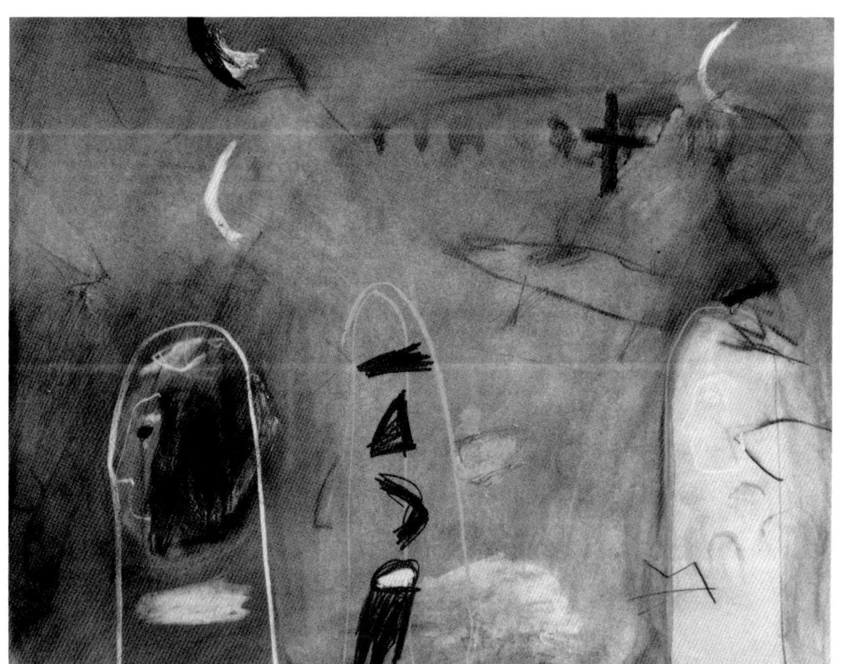

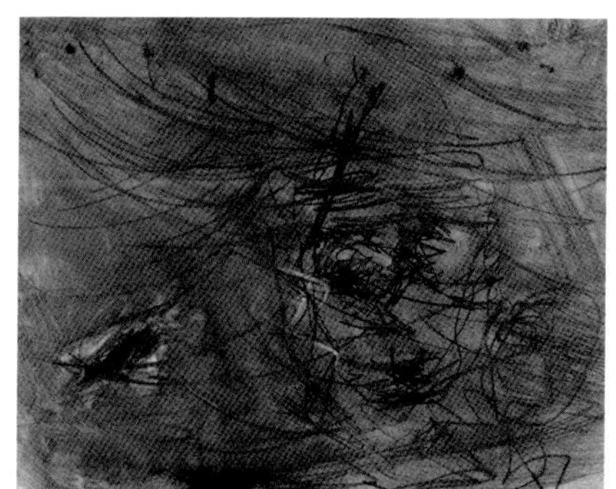

Untitled, 1975
Mixed media on paper
21¾ x 27¾"
Collection Timothy Stack, Houston

Untitled, 1976
Mixed media on paper
10¼ x 13¼"
Collection George Krause, Houston

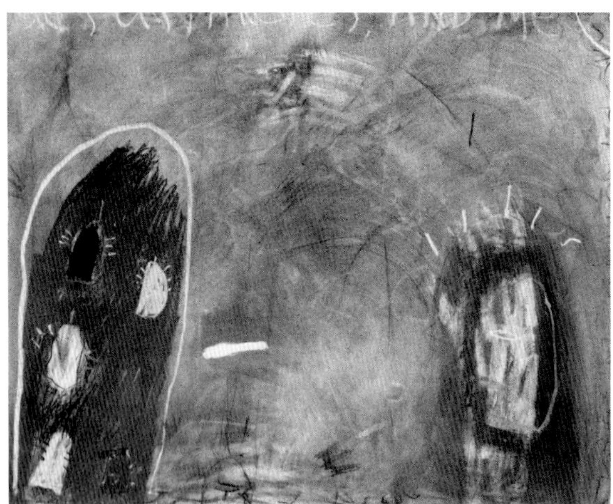

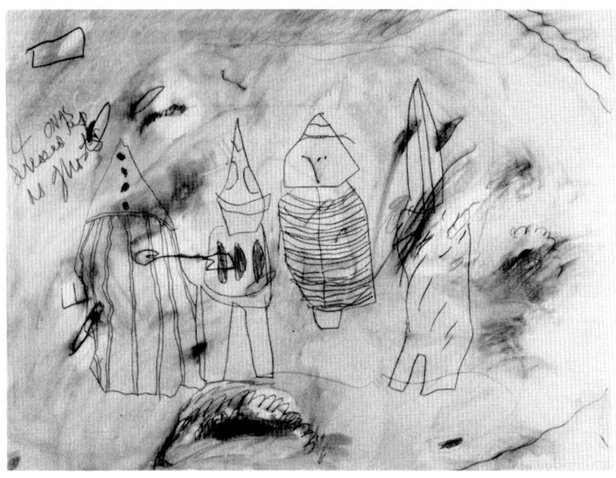

Up Against the Wall, 1976
Chalk, pencil and Cray-pas on paper
23 x 29"
Collection Solomon R. Guggenheim Museum,
New York
Exxon Corporation Purchase Award, 1981

Four Onas Dressed Up as Ghosts, 1976
Mixed media on paper
28 x 38"
Collection Mr. and Mrs. John Wilson Kelsey,
Houston

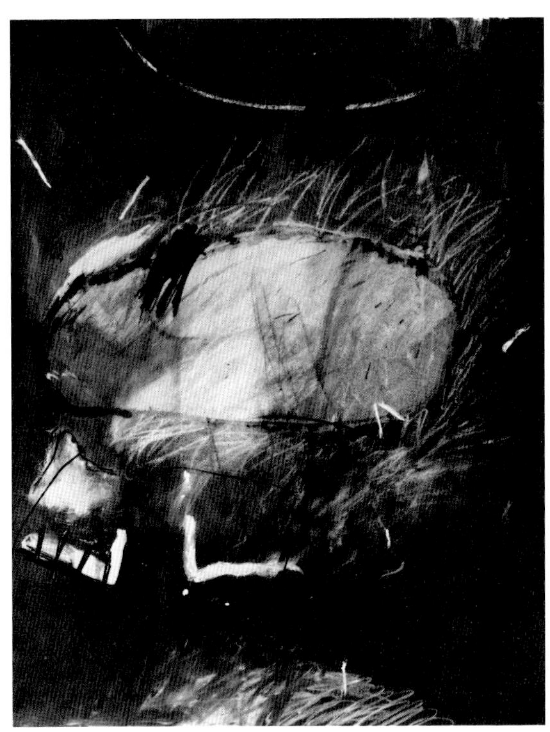

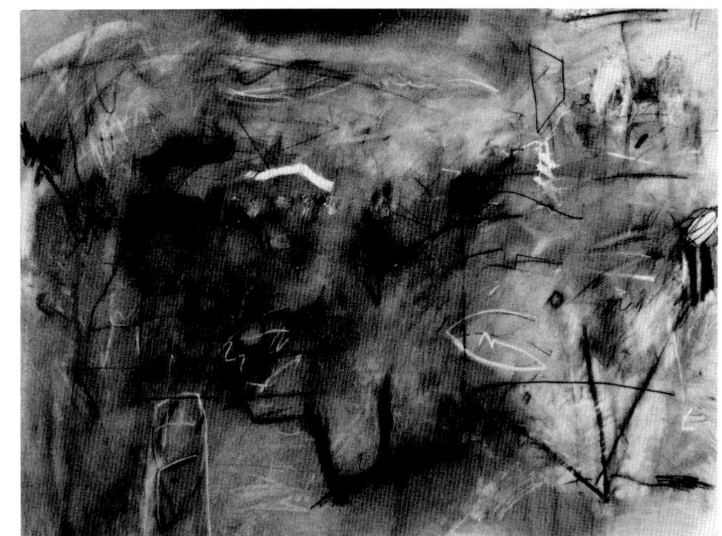

Untitled, 1977
Mixed media on paper
27¾ x 22"
Collection Charlotte Cosgrove, Houston

Helen's Dream, 1978
Pastel, graphite and oil on paper
27¾ x 37½"
Collection Balene McCormick, Houston

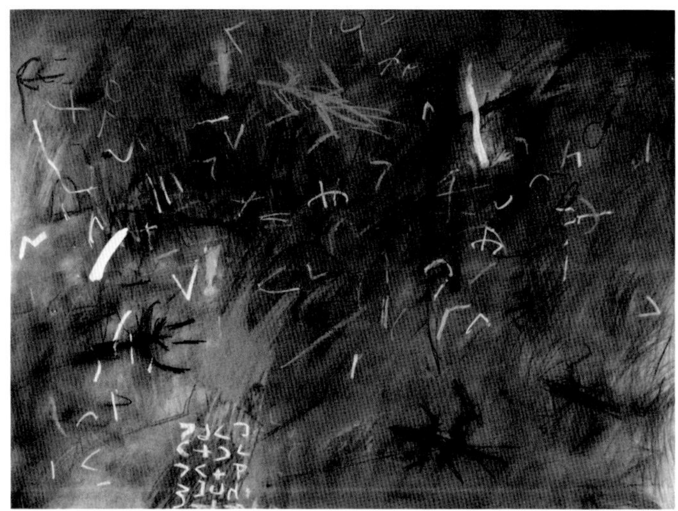

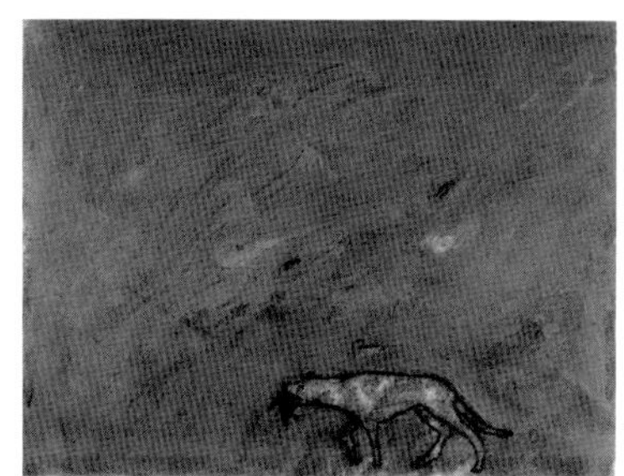

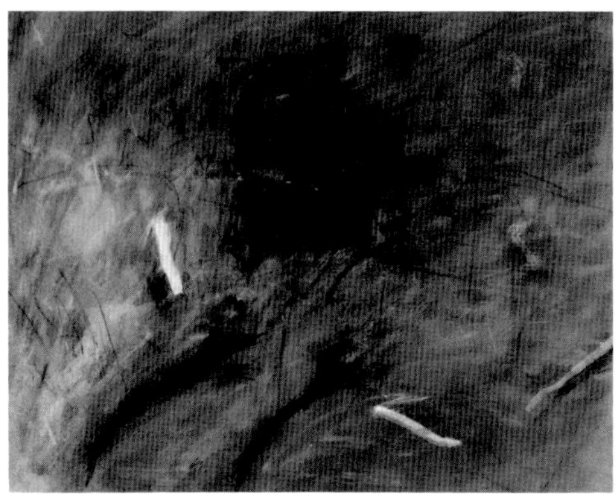

Untitled, 1977
Mixed media on paper
27¾ x 37⅞"
Collection Mr. and Mrs. A. L. Ballard, Houston

Untitled (Birthday Drawing), 1978
Mixed media on paper
20⅞ x 27"
Collection Todd and Marianne Pomeroy, Dallas

Untitled, 1978
Mixed media on paper
10¼ x 13¼"
Collection Janie C. Lee, Houston

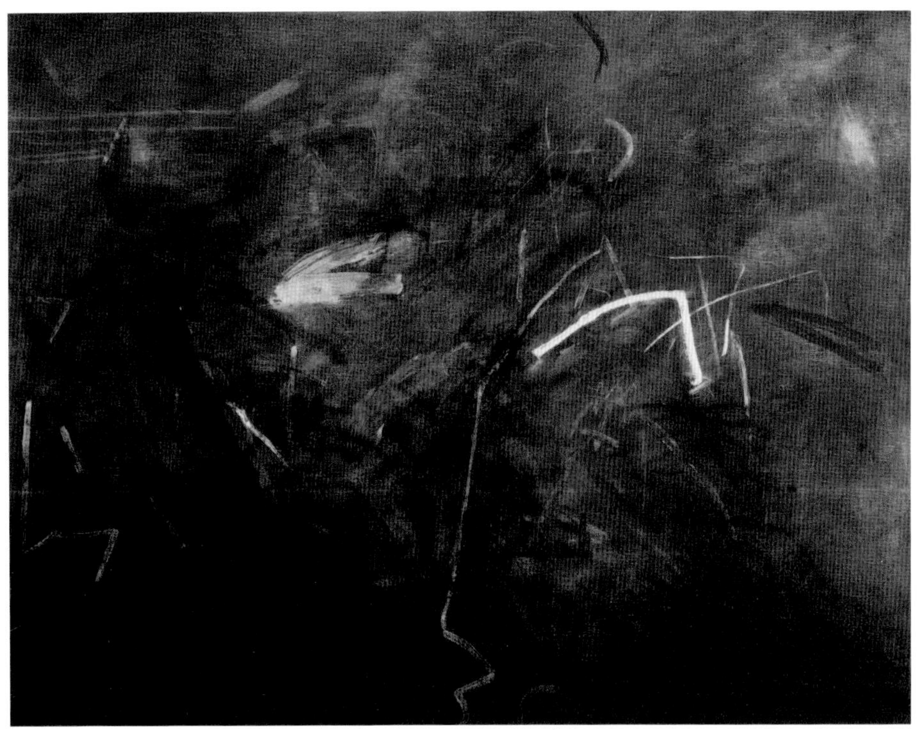

Untitled, 1979
Oil on canvas
40 x 52"
Collection George Bunker, Houston

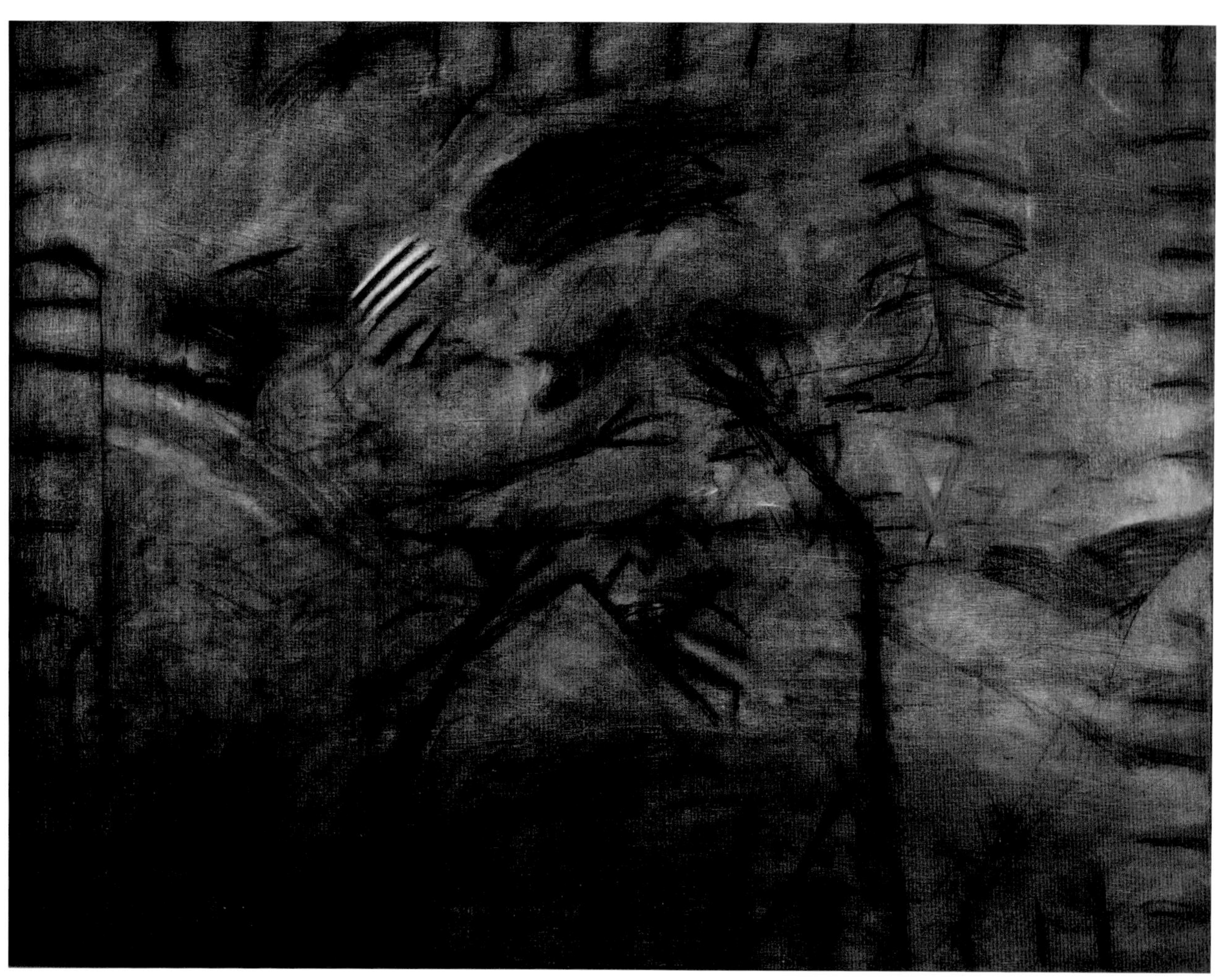

**St. John in the Wilderness, after
di Paolo (for Sandra)**, 1980
Oil on canvas
40 x 52"
Collection Sandra and Bubba Levy, Houston

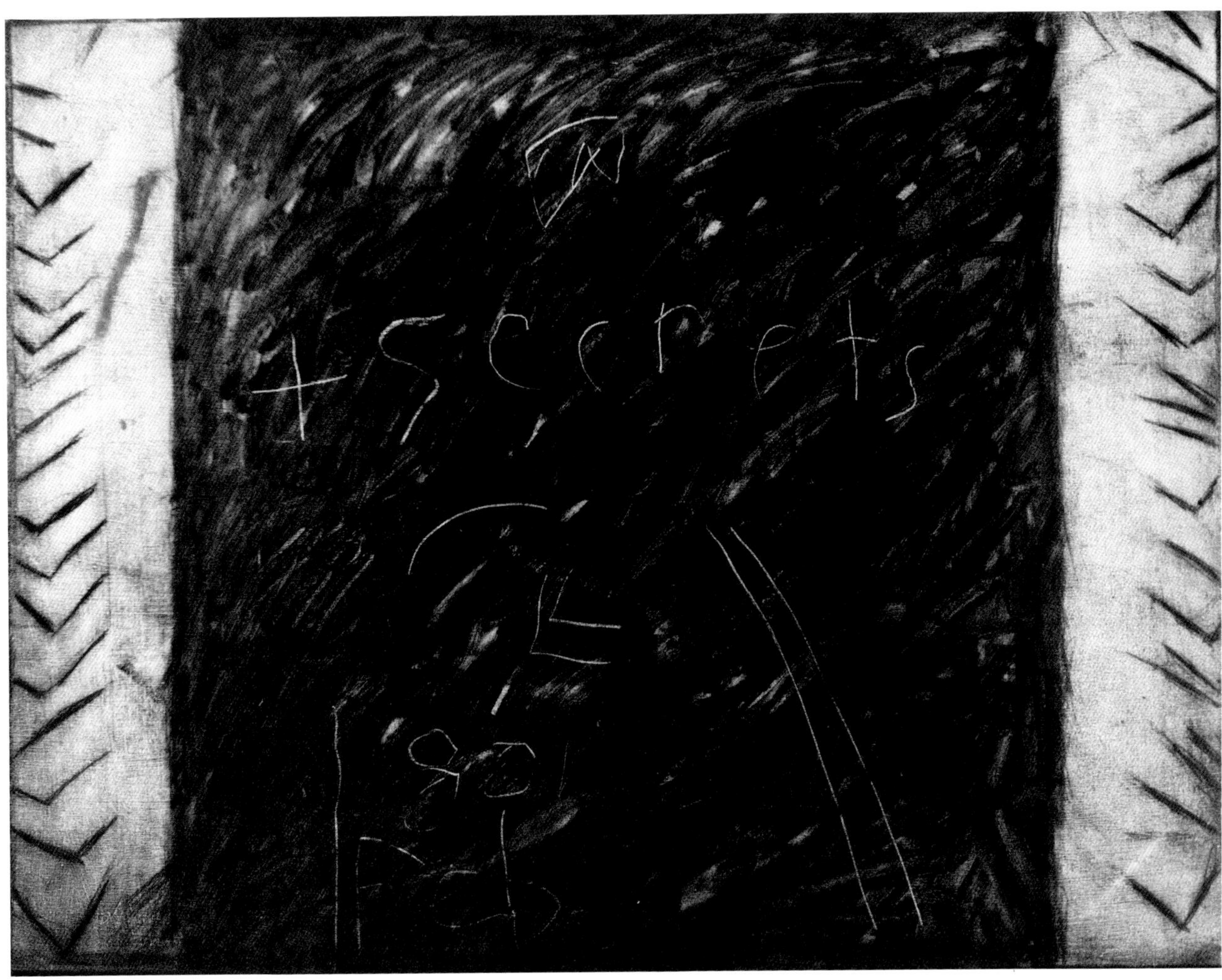

Secrets, 1980
Oil on canvas
40 x 52"
Collection Ed Hill and Suzanne Bloom, Houston

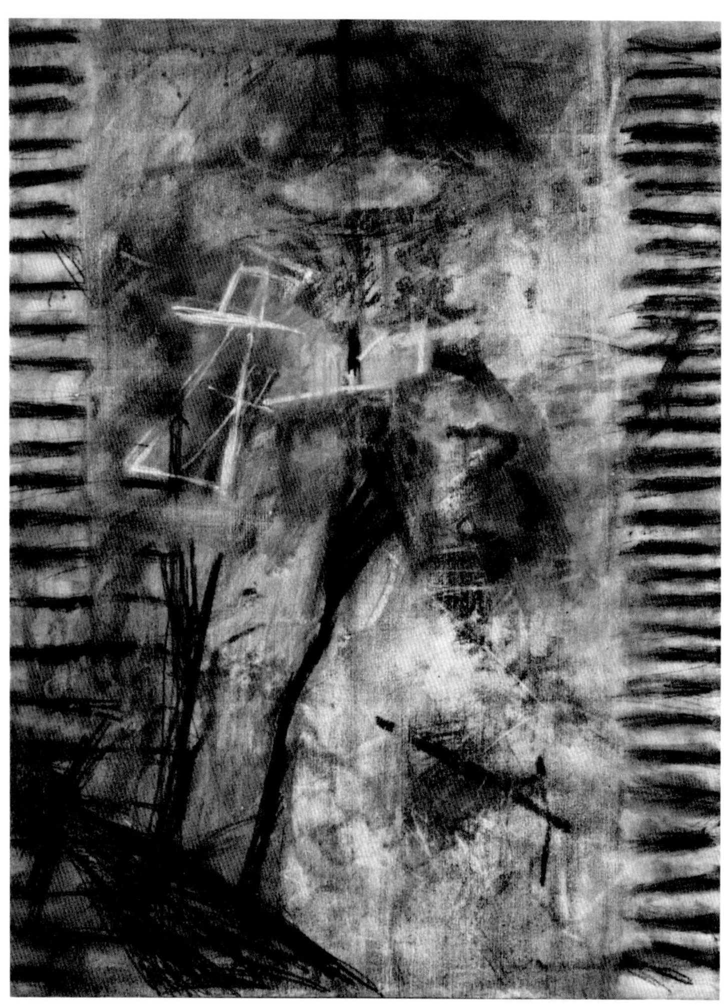

Untitled (for Ensor), 1981
Mixed media on canvas
40 x 30"
Collection Benjamin C. Crump, Houston

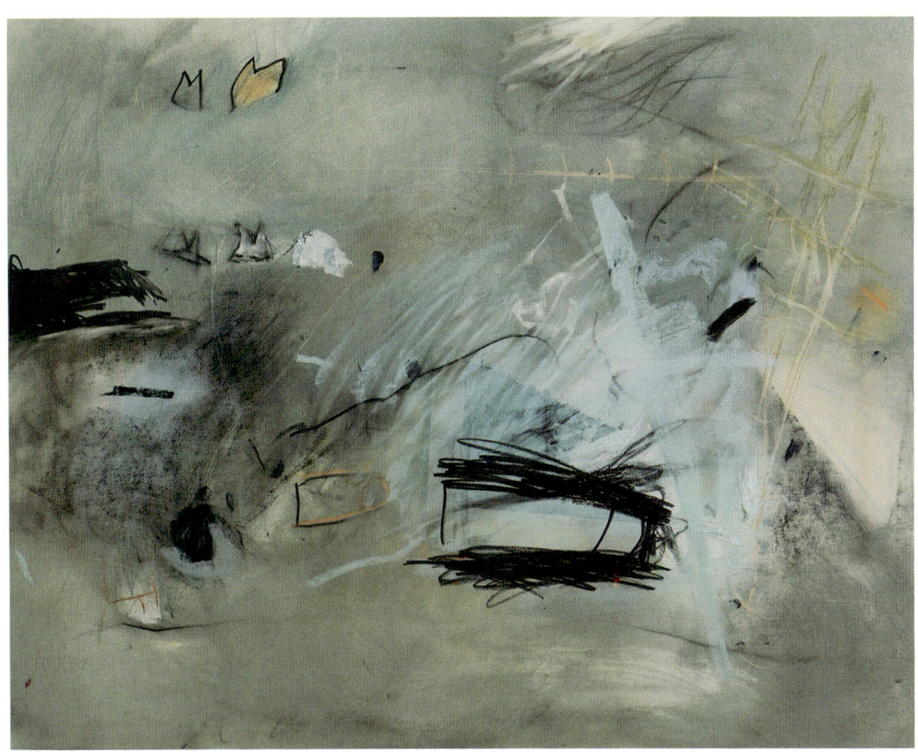

Untitled, 1976
Mixed media on paper
21¾ x 27¾"
Collection George Bunker, Houston

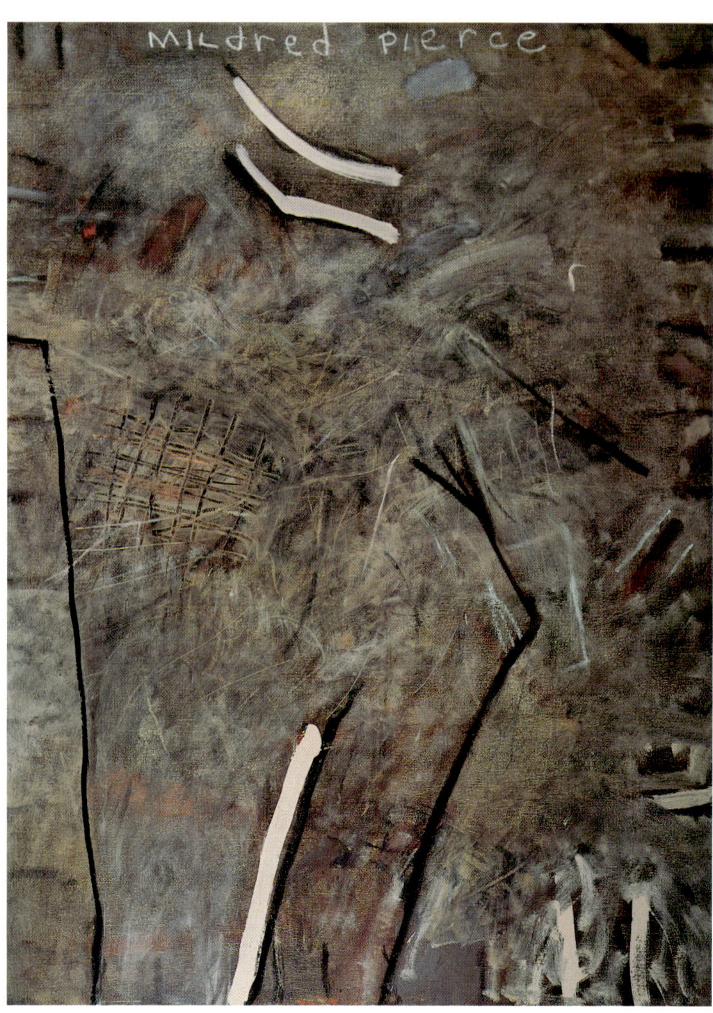

Mildred Pierce, 1978
Oil on canvas
56 x 42"
Private collection

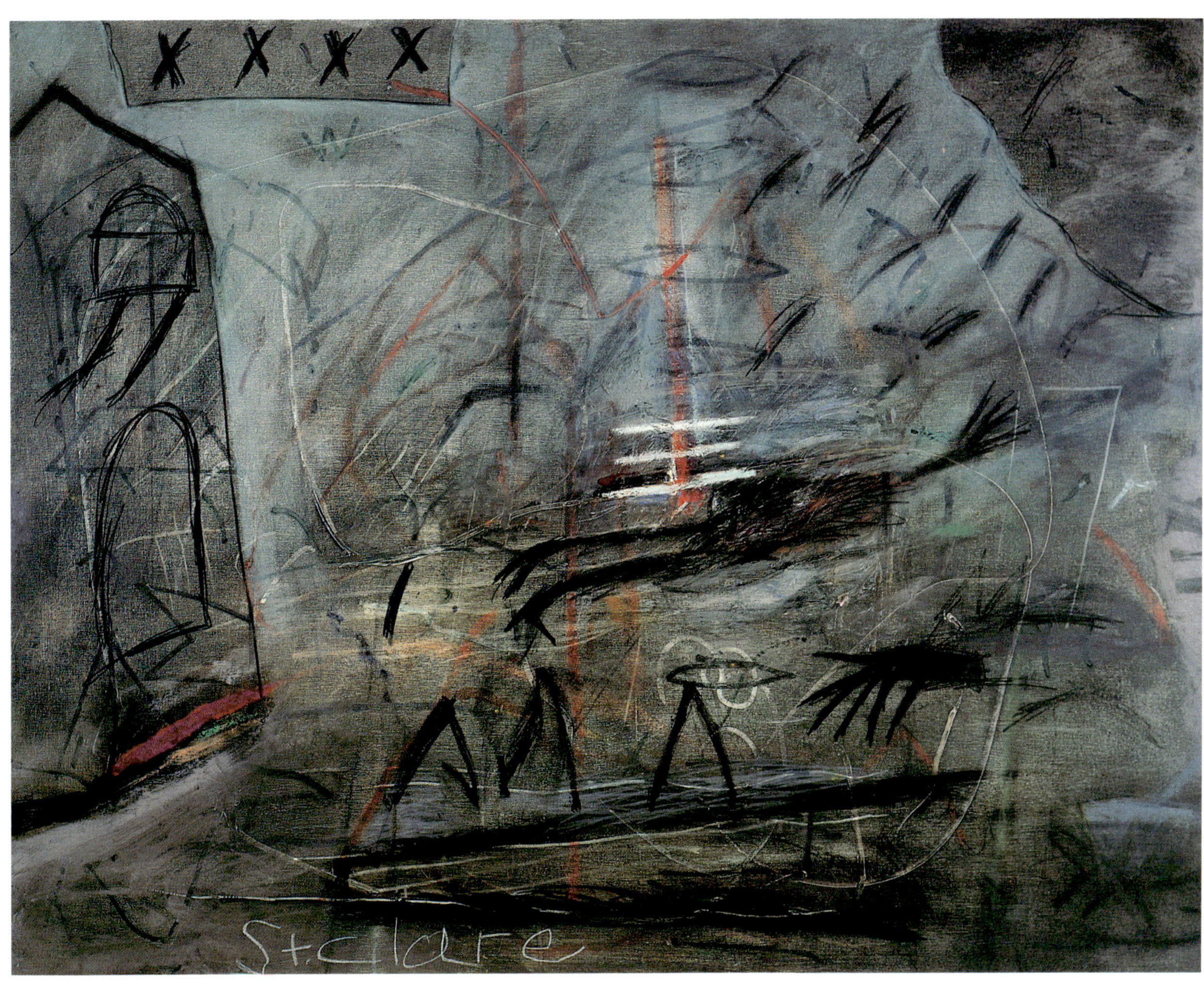

**St. Clare Saving a Child Being Mauled by
a Wolf, after Giovanni di Paolo**, 1980
Oil on canvas
40 x 52″
Collection Bob Wilson, Houston

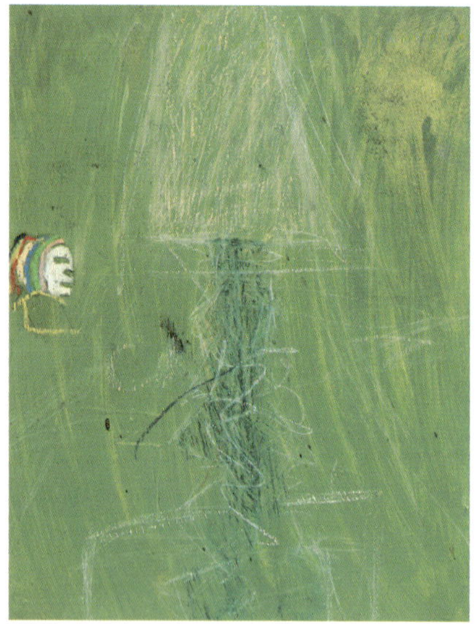

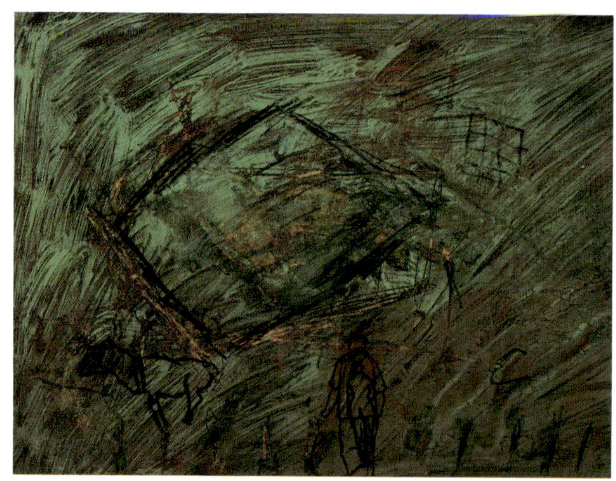

Untitled, 1982
Mixed media on paper
12¼ x 9½"
Collection Mrs. Sue R. Pittman, Houston

Untitled (for Paul), 1982
Oil and graphite on paper
9⅞ x 12⅝"
Collection Sandra and Bubba Levy, Houston

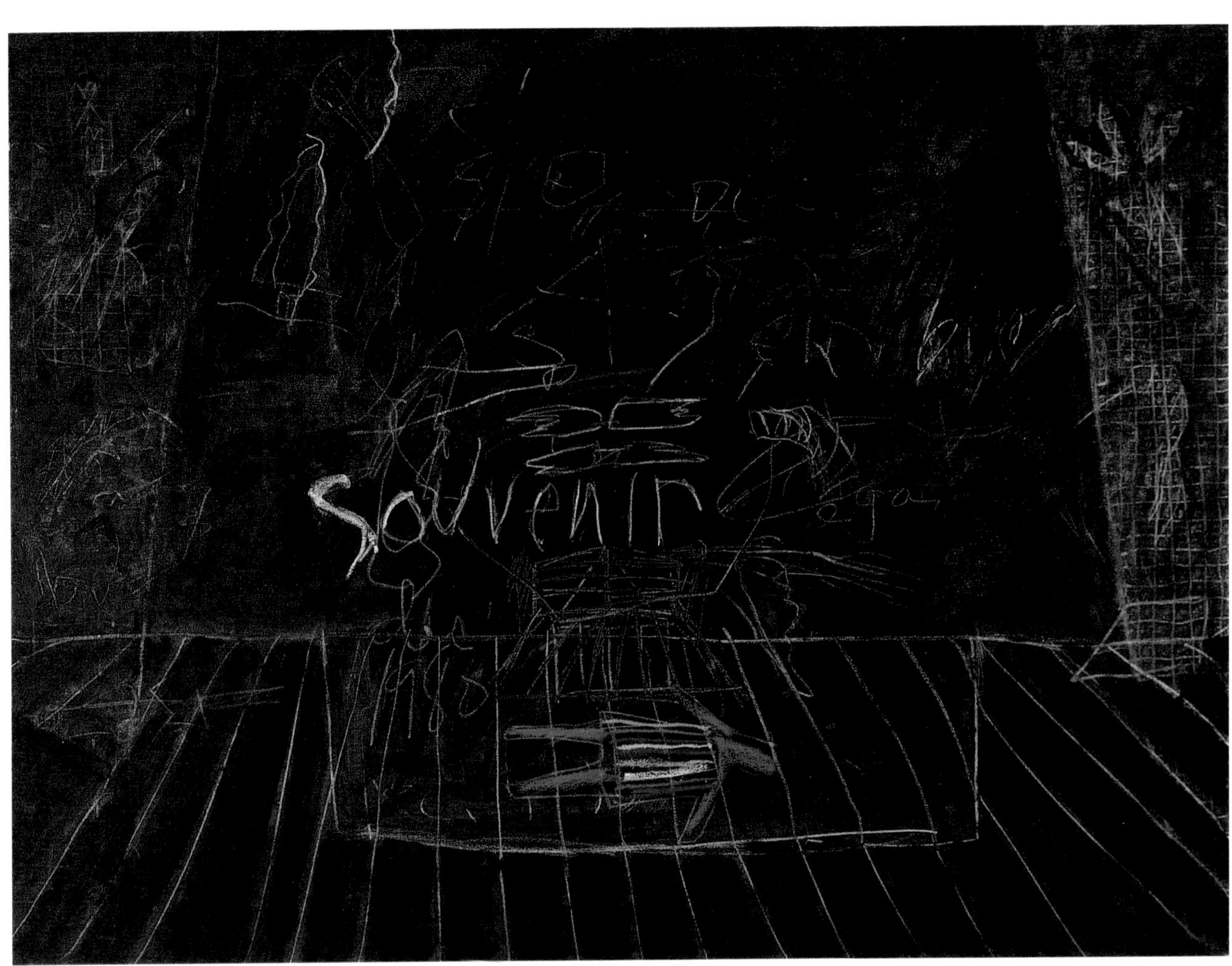

Souvenir (The Anton Christian Painting), 1980
Oil on canvas
30 x 40"
Collection Wilson Industries, Inc., Houston

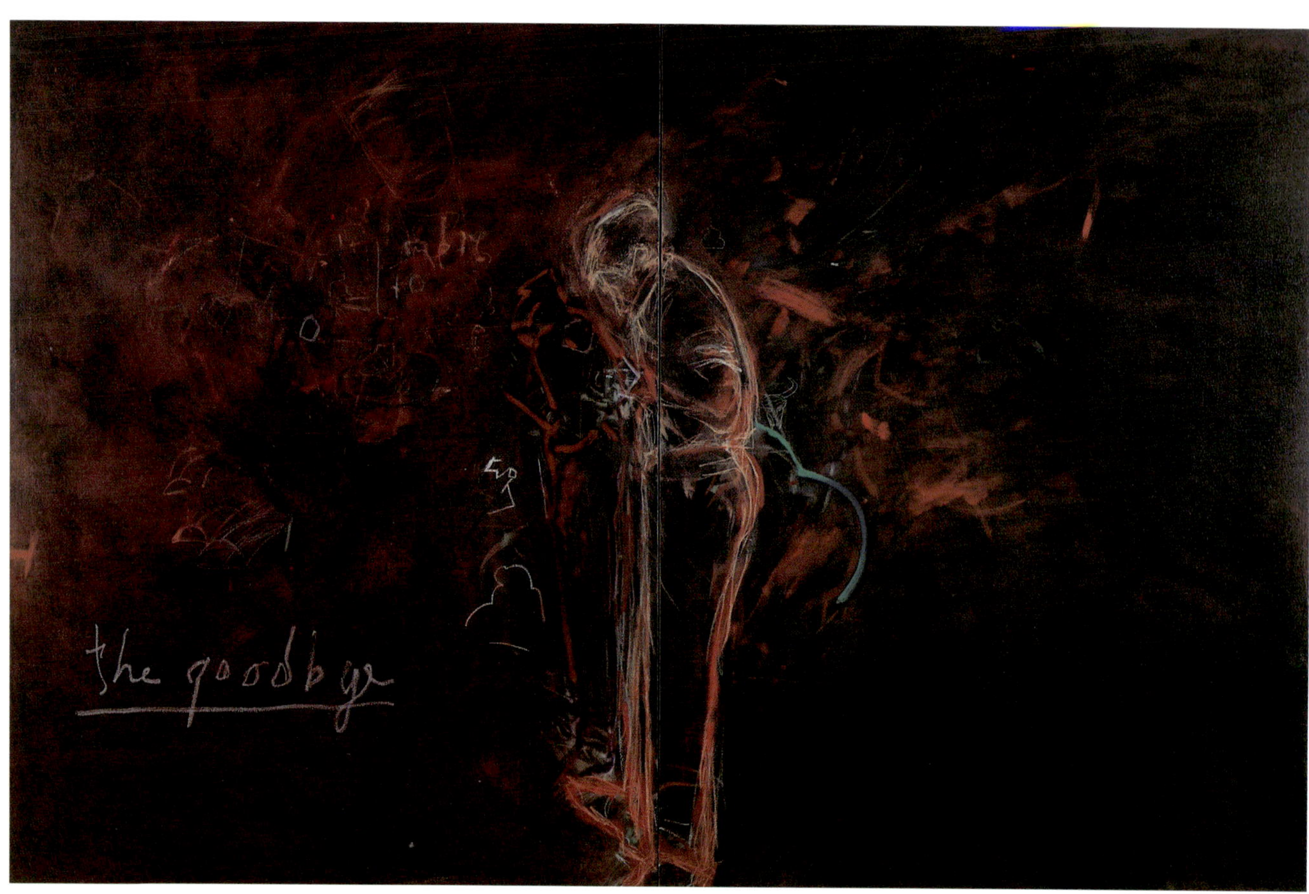

The Goodbye, 1983
Oil on canvas
Two panels, each 52¼ x 40¼″
Collection Mayor Day & Caldwell, Houston

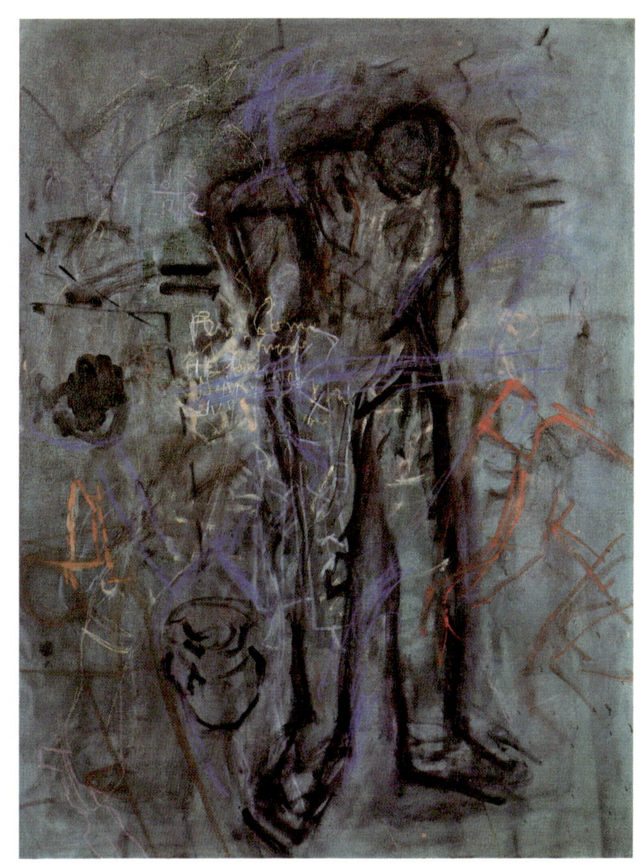

Lesson 3 (for Janie), 1984
Oil on canvas
50 x 42"
Collection Judy and Donald Bredenburgh,
New York

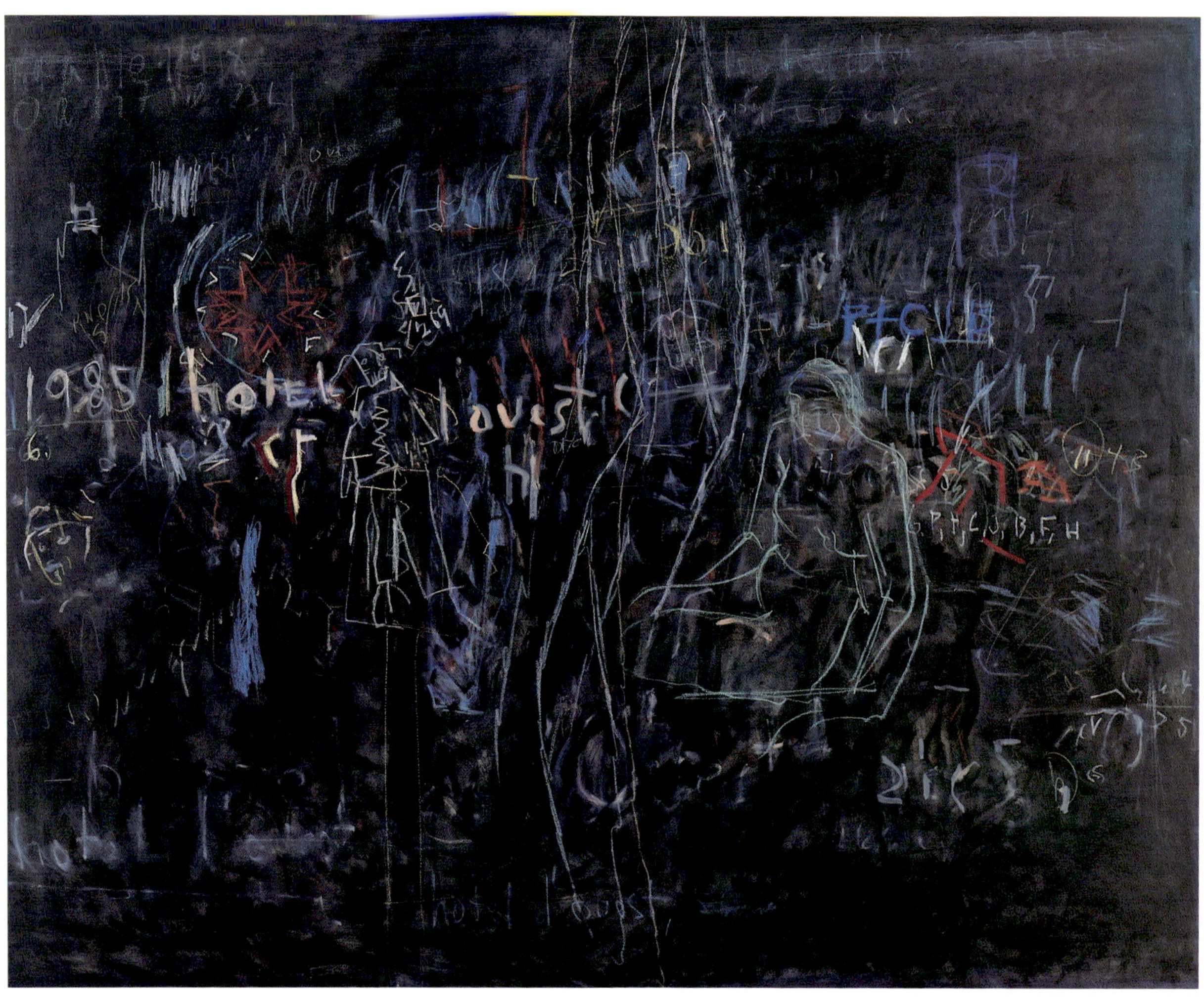

Hôtel de l'ouest, 1985
Oil on canvas
60 x 76"
Courtesy David Beitzel Gallery, New York, and
Moody Gallery, Houston

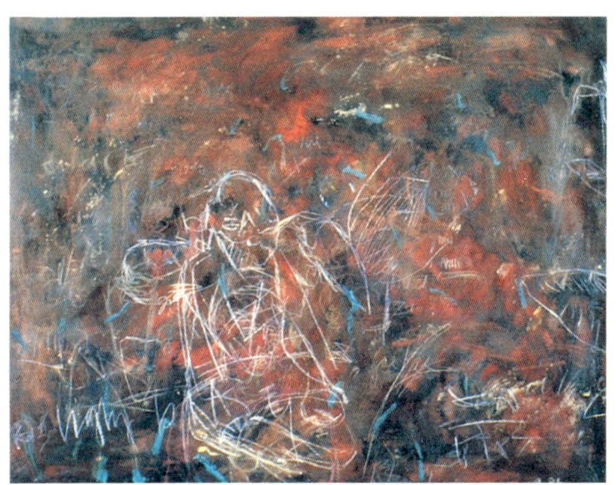

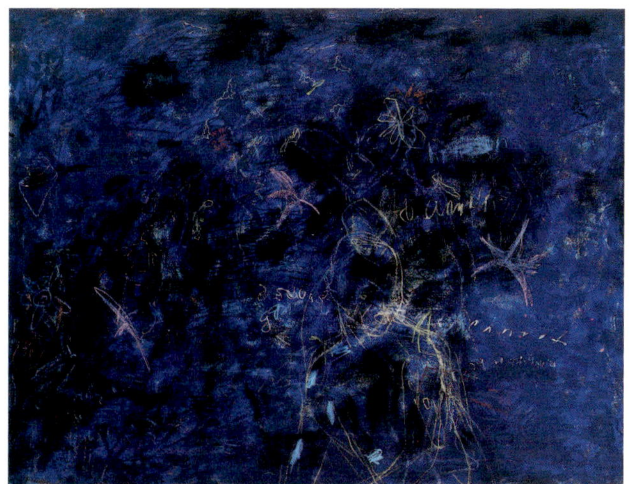

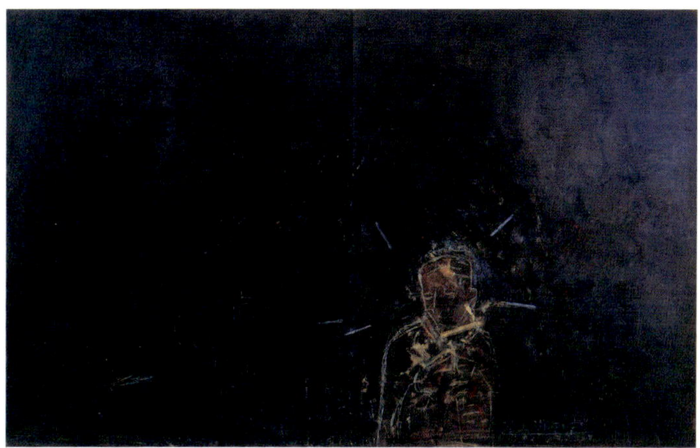

Ugly Patsy, 1987
Oll on paper
23 x 29"
Collection Nancy M. O'Boyle, Dallas

Untitled, 1989
Mixed media on lithograph
29⅞ x 40"
Courtesy the artist and Houston Fine
Art Press

Hackney, 1986
Mixed media on paper
27 x 44"
Collection Helen Elizabeth Hill Trust, Houston

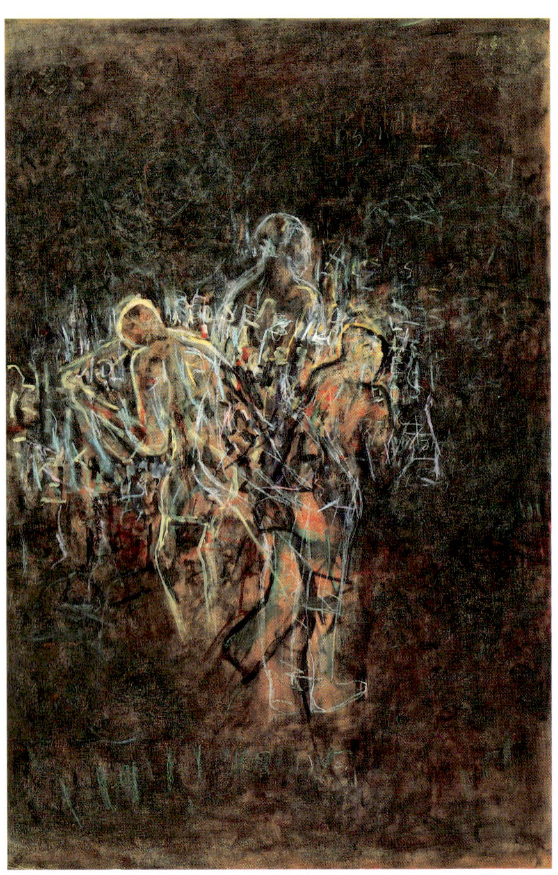

Rose's Last Summer, 1985
Oil on canvas
62¼ x 48¹⁄₁₆"
Collection Dallas Museum of Art

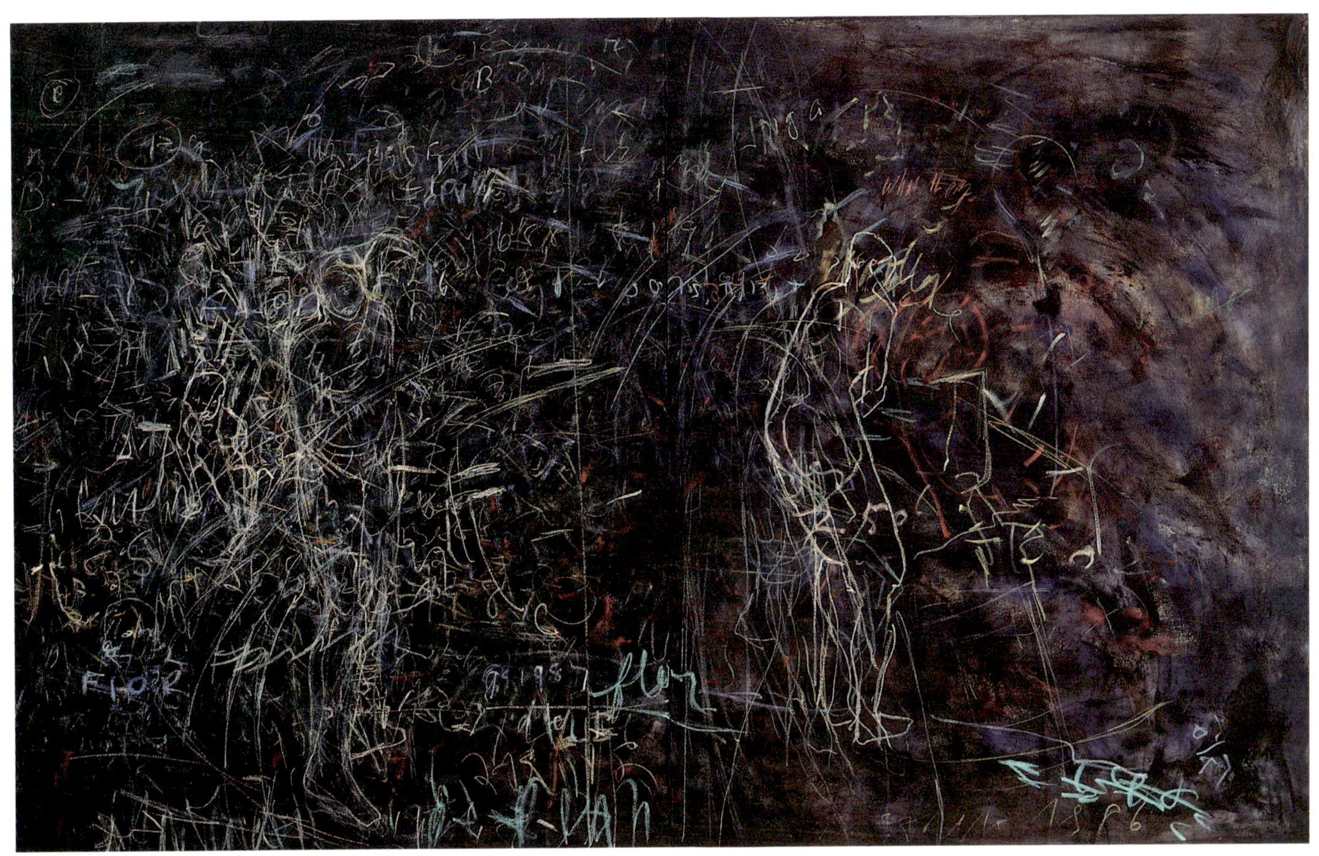

Flor, 1987
Oil on canvas
Two panels, each 60 x 48″
Collection Balene McCormick, Houston

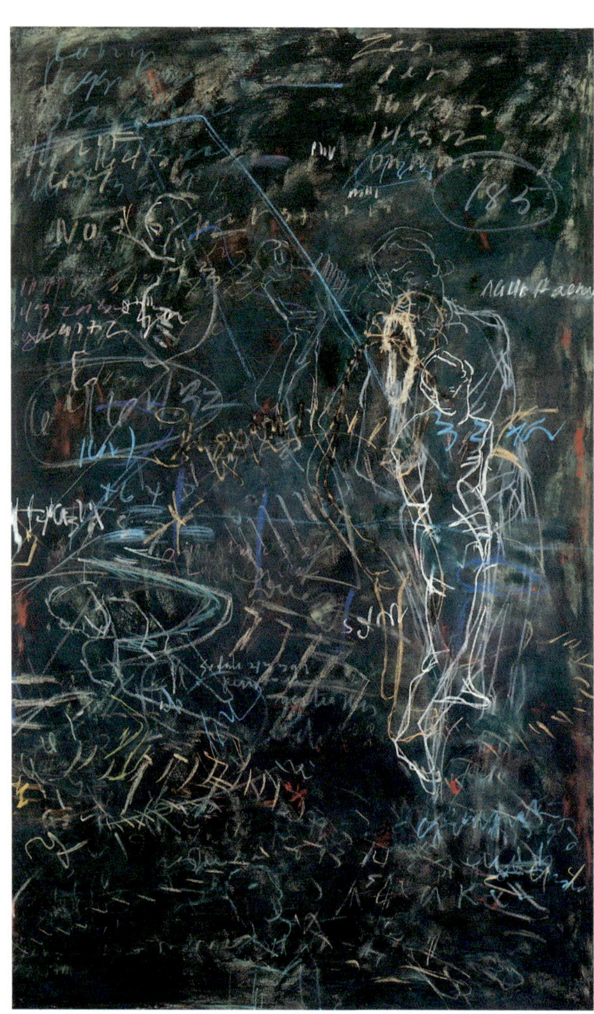

Mild Warnings, 1987
Oil on canvas
77 x 48"
Collection Progressive Corporation,
Mayfield Heights, Ohio

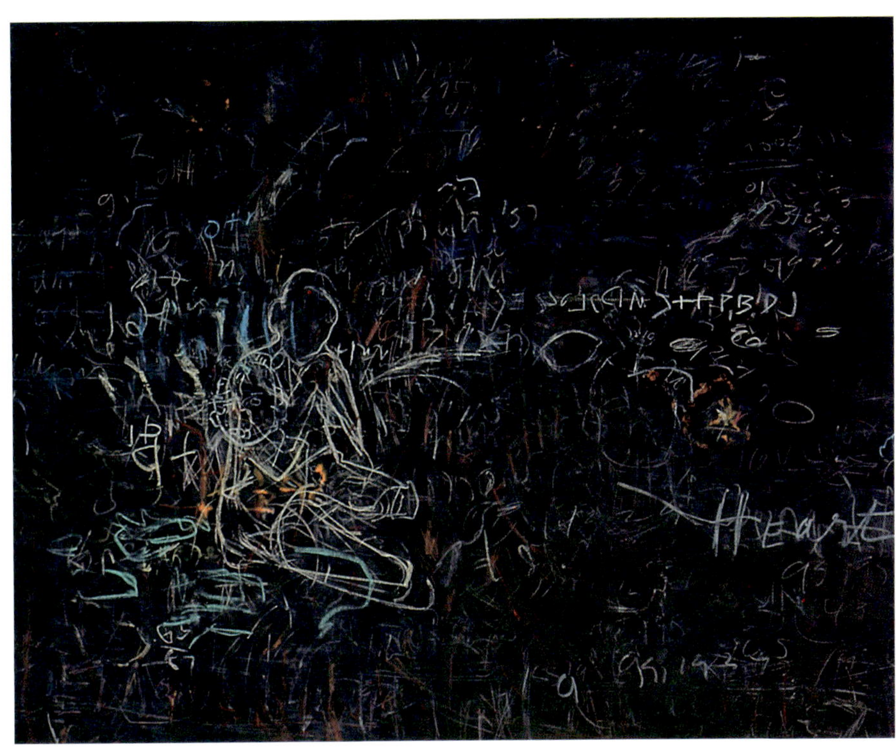

Lemon Heart, 1987
Oil on canvas
48 x 60″
Private collection, New York

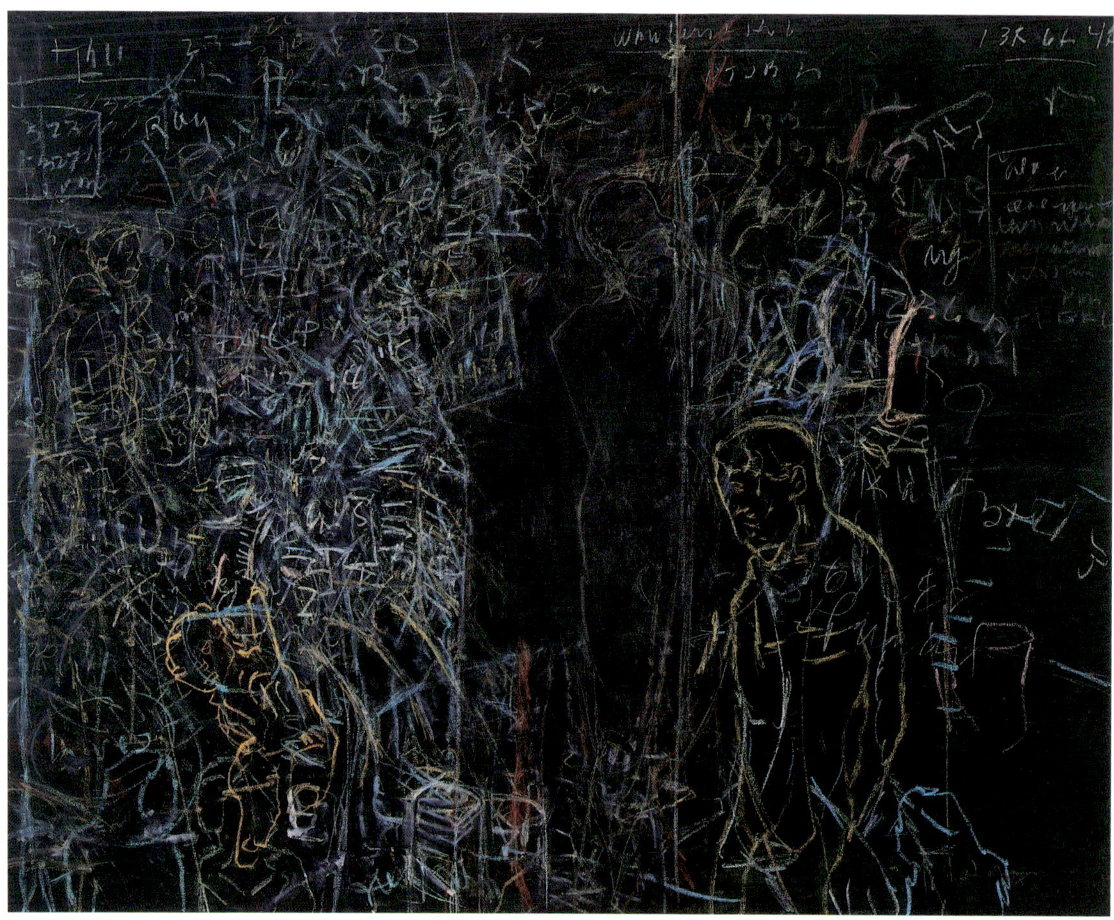

Untitled, 1987-88
Oil on canvas
60 x 76"
Courtesy David Beitzel Gallery, New York, and
Moody Gallery, Houston

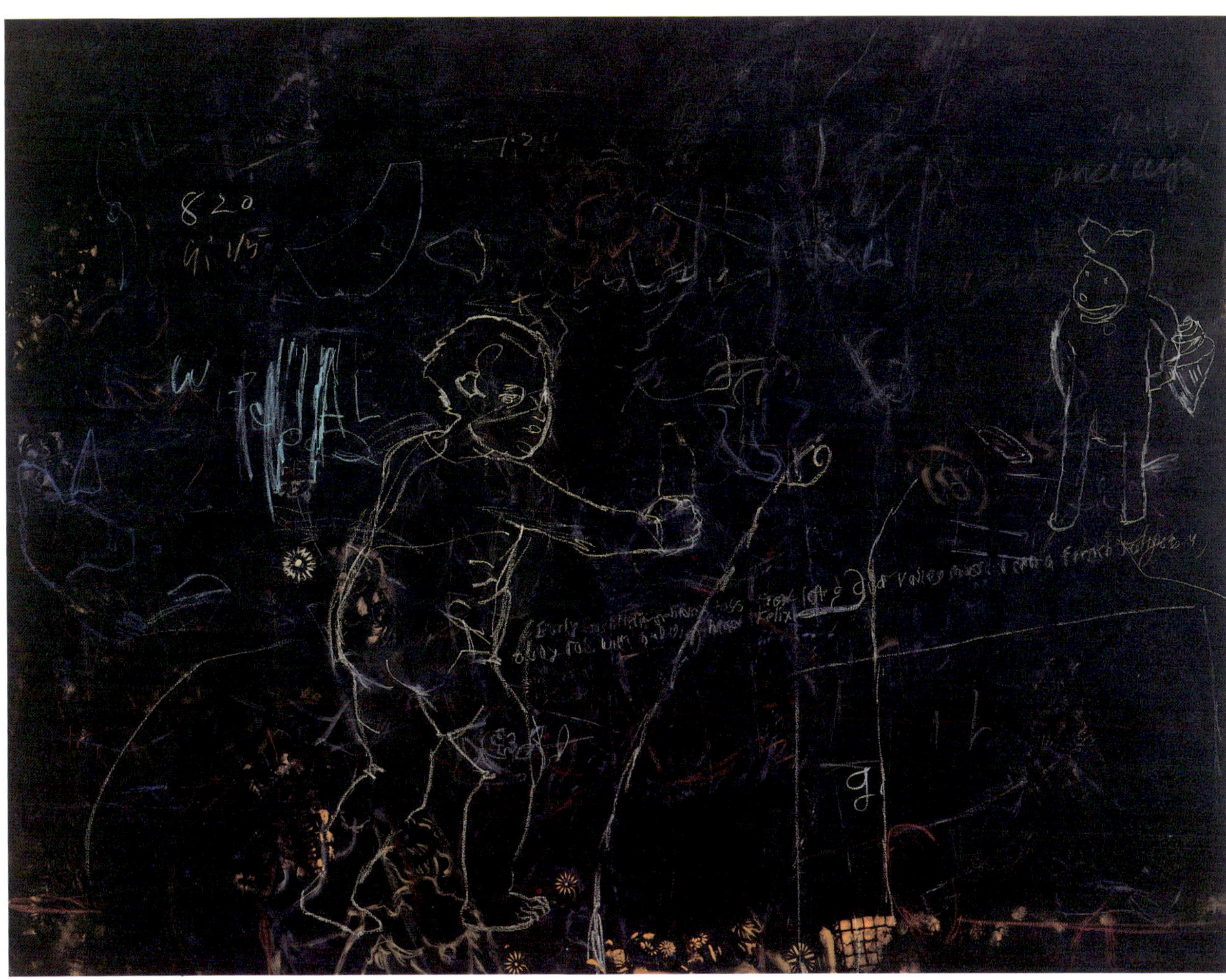

Bill, 1988
Oil on canvas
64 x 84"
Courtesy David Beitzel Gallery, New York, and
Moody Gallery, Houston

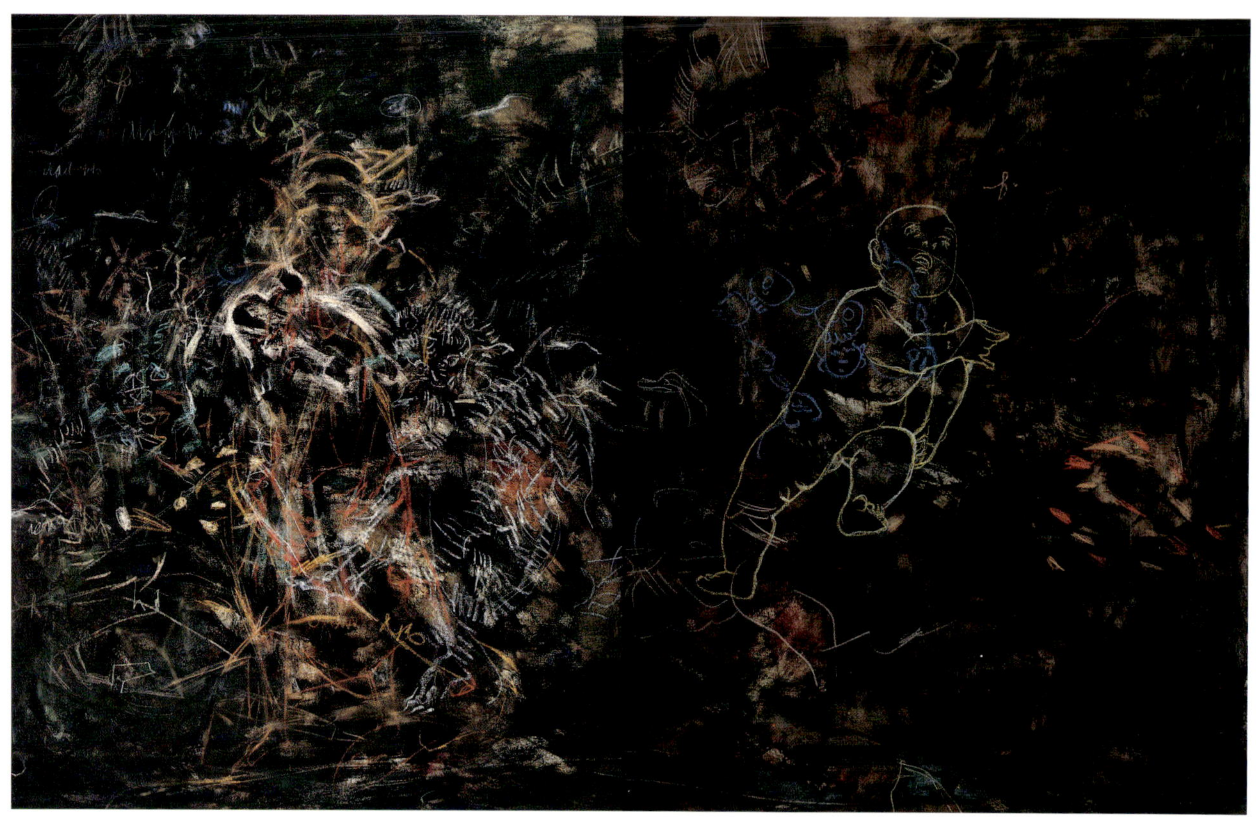

Untitled, 1989
Oil on canvas
Two panels, each 60 x 48"
Courtesy Janie C. Lee Gallery, Houston and
New York, and Moody Gallery, Houston

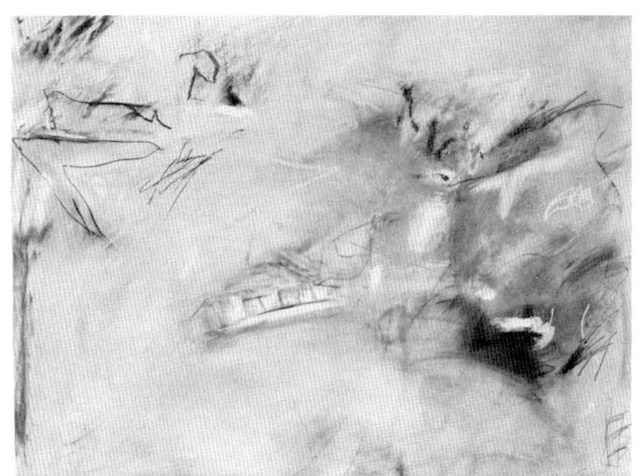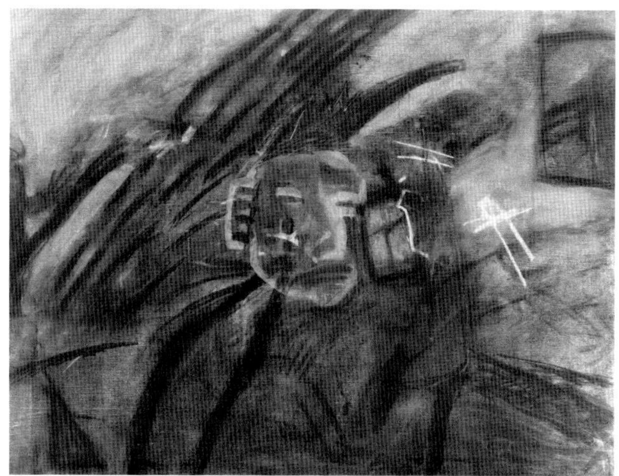

Central Adjustment Bureau, 1980
Mixed media on paper
30 x 40"
Collection The Gihon Foundation, Dallas

Untitled, 1981
Mixed media on canvas
30 x 40"
Collection Joan H. Fleming, Houston

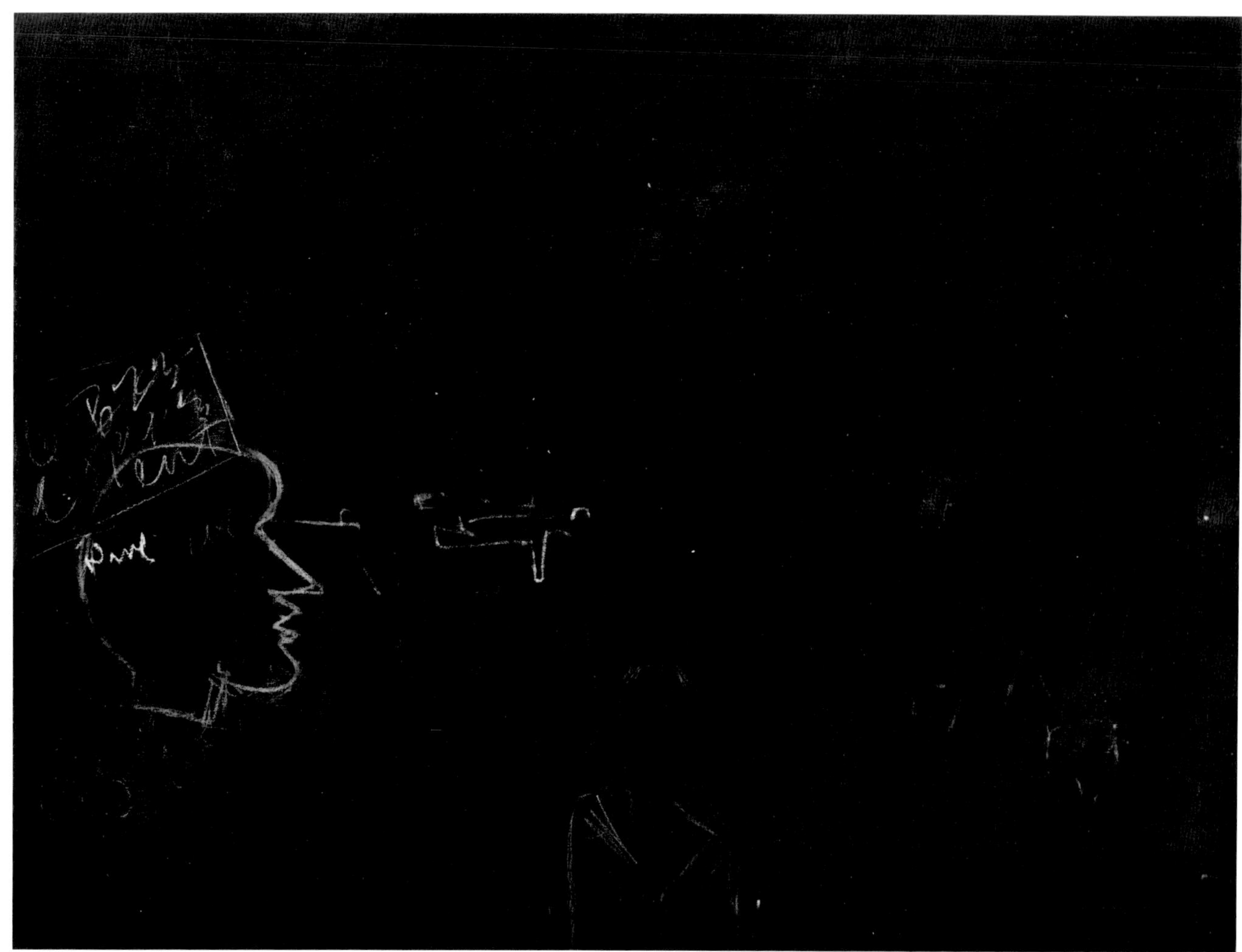

Call Maureen, 1982
Oil on canvas
36 x 48"
Collection Betty Moody and Bill Steffy,
Houston

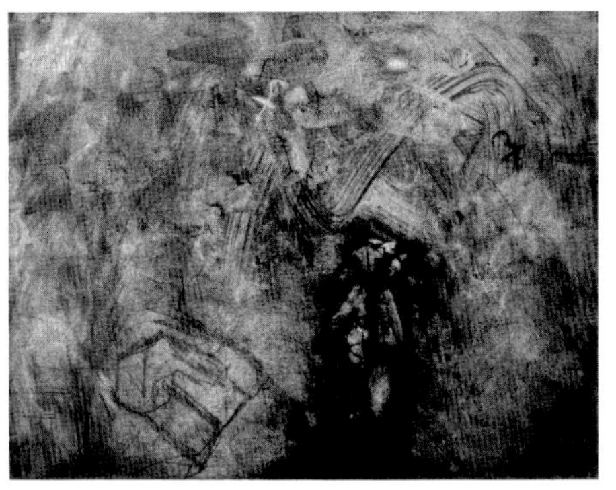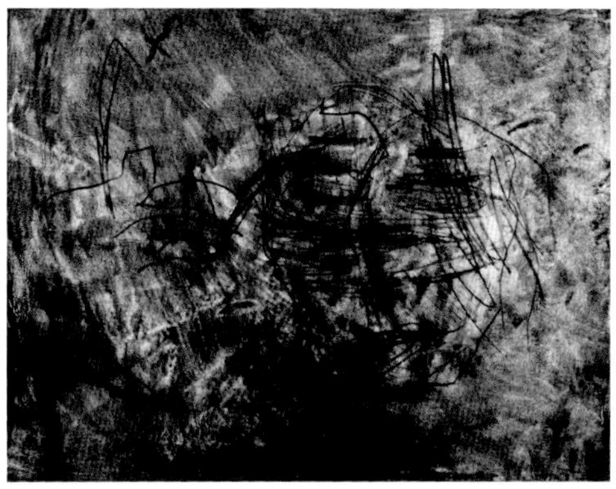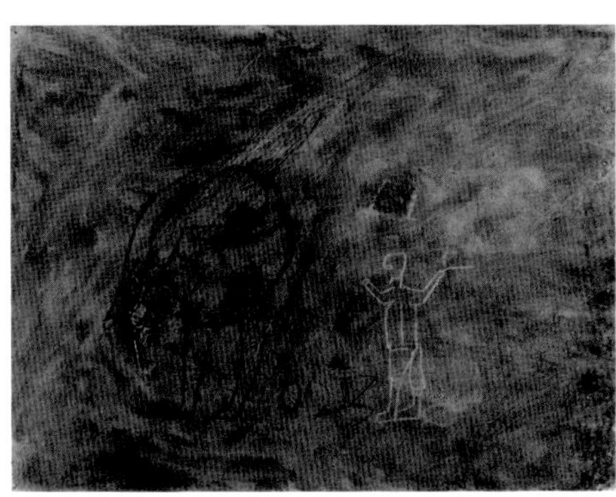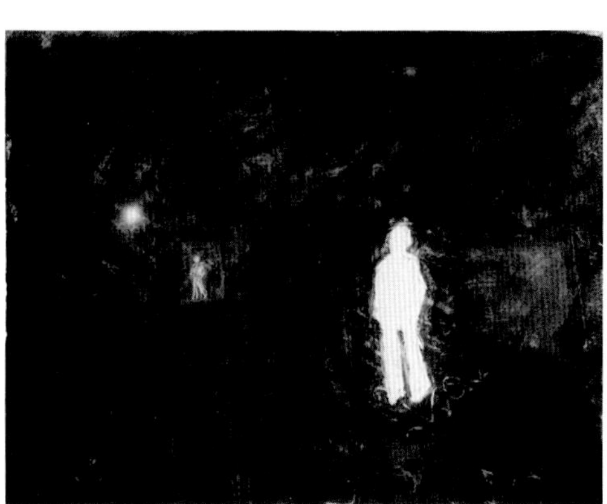

Untitled (Gael Stack at the Guggenheim), 1981
Oil and graphite on paper
10¼ x 13"
Anonymous loan

Self-Portrait with Adolescent Son, 1982
Oil on paper
10½ x 13½"
Collection Sandra and Bubba Levy, Houston

Untitled, 1981
Mixed media on paper
11¼ x 14"
Collection Jinny and Harrison Itz, Houston

Untitled, 1982
Mixed media on paper
11¼ x 14"
Collection Jinny and Harrison Itz, Houston

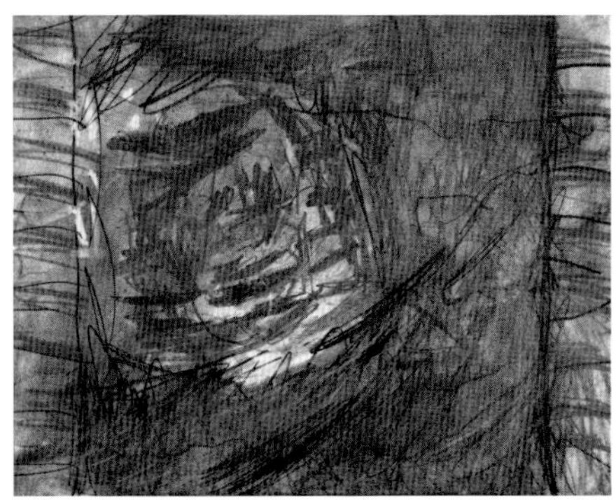
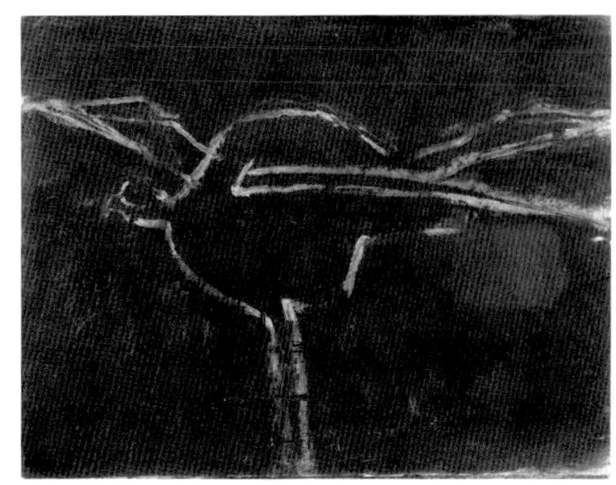
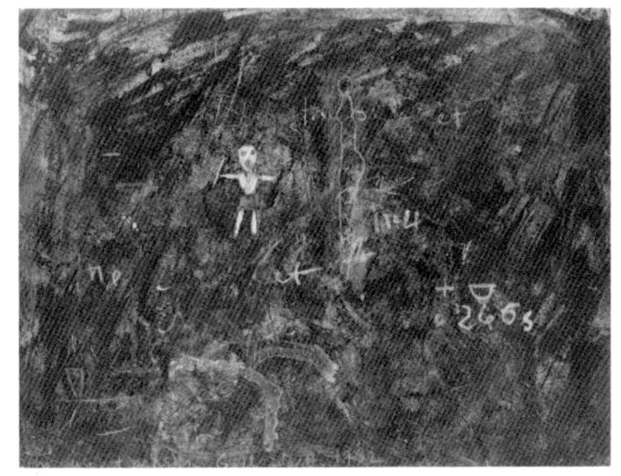
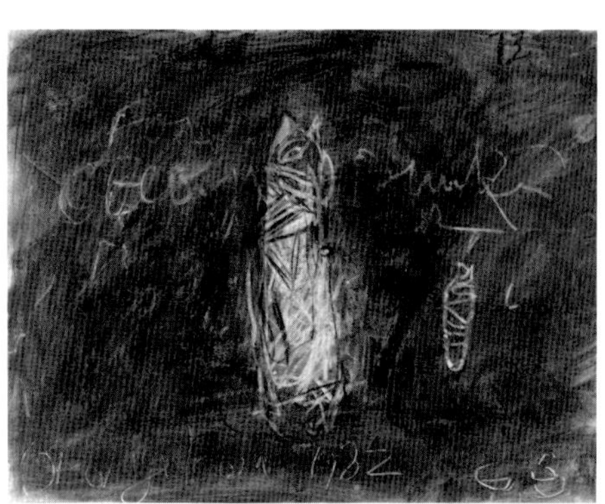

Untitled, 1981
Mixed media on paper
11½ x 14½"
Collection Lucas and Patricia C. Johnson,
Houston

Untitled, 1982
Mixed media on paper
10¾ x 14"
Collection Paula Webb, Houston

The Suspect Person, 1982
Oil on paper
11⅝ x 14⅝"
Colection Transco Energy Company, Houston

Untitled (Mummified Cat), 1982
Mixed media on paper
9½ x 12½"
Collection George Bunker, Houston

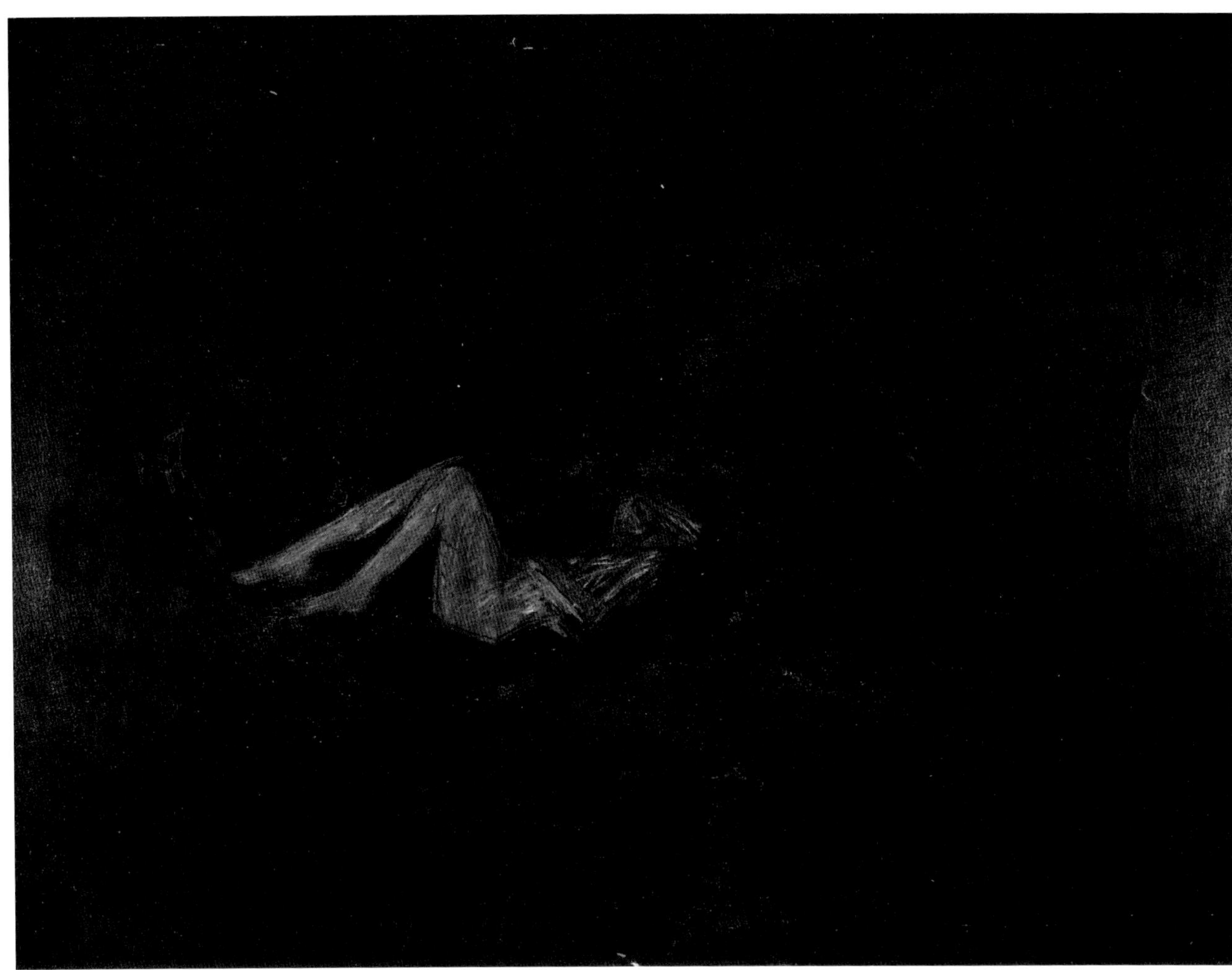

The Disquieting Object, 1983
Oil on canvas
38¼ x 50¼"
Courtesy Janie C. Lee Gallery, Houston and
New York, and Moody Gallery, Houston

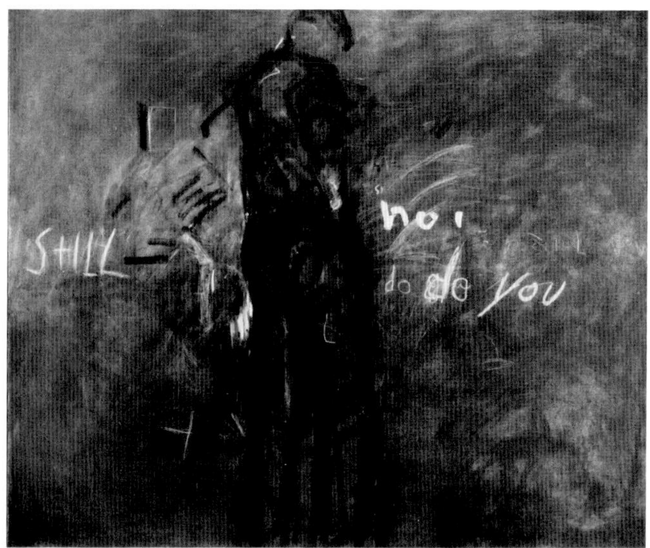

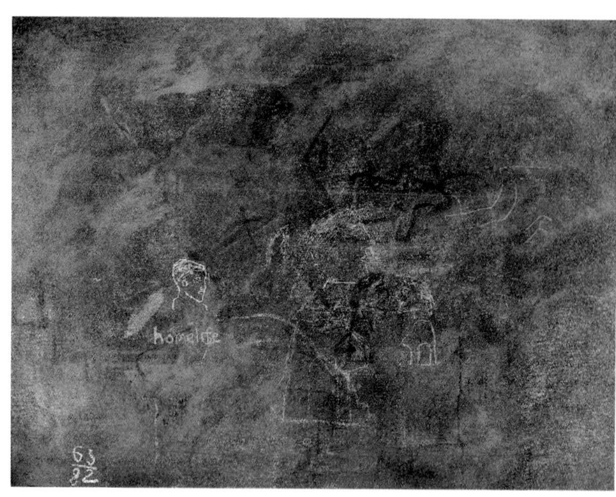

The Correspondence, 1983
Oil on canvas
48 x 58½"
Courtesy Janie C. Lee Gallery, Houston and
New York, and Moody Gallery, Houston

Homelife, 1982
Oil on canvas
40 x 52"
Collection The Museum of Fine Arts, Houston
Museum purchase with funds provided by
the National Endowment for the Arts and
Mrs. William H. Lane

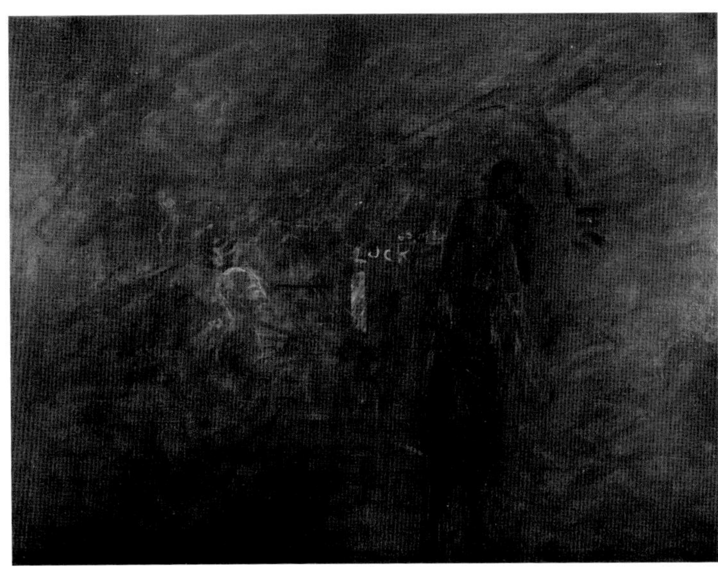

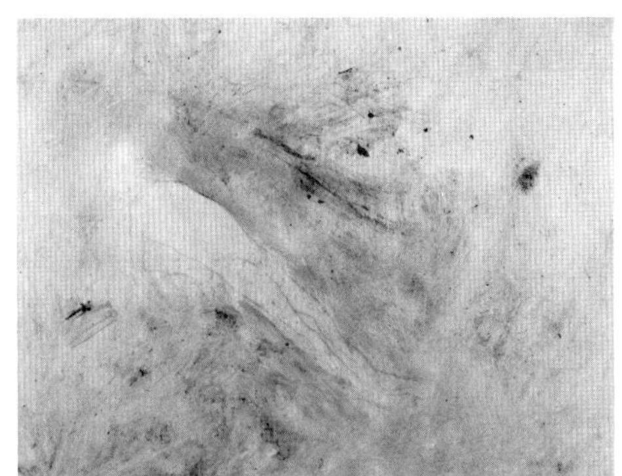

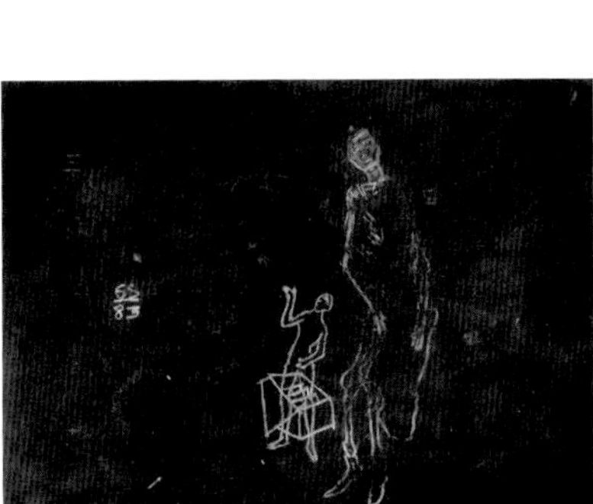

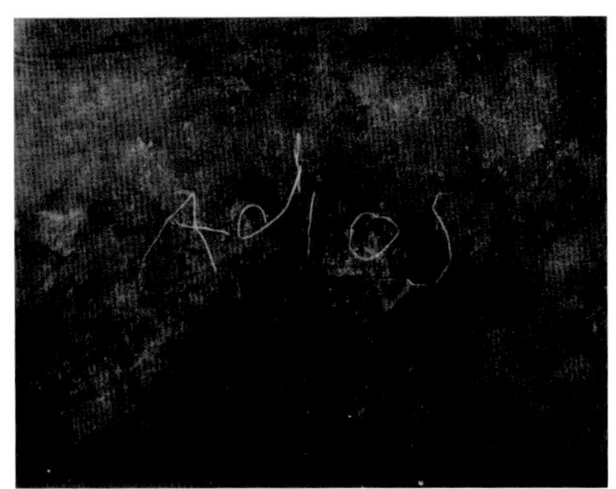

Luck, 1983
Oil and pencil on canvas
41¾ x 53½"
Collection Alicia Talley and Allan Smith,
San Francisco

For Miss Brave America, 1983
Mixed media on paper
9⅞ x 12⅞"
Collection Todd and Marianne Pomeroy, Dallas

Untitled, 1983
Mixed media on paper
9¾ x 12¾"
Collection Alan and Martha Farrington,
Houston

Adios, 1983
Oil on paper
10 x 13"
Collection Balene McCormick, Houston

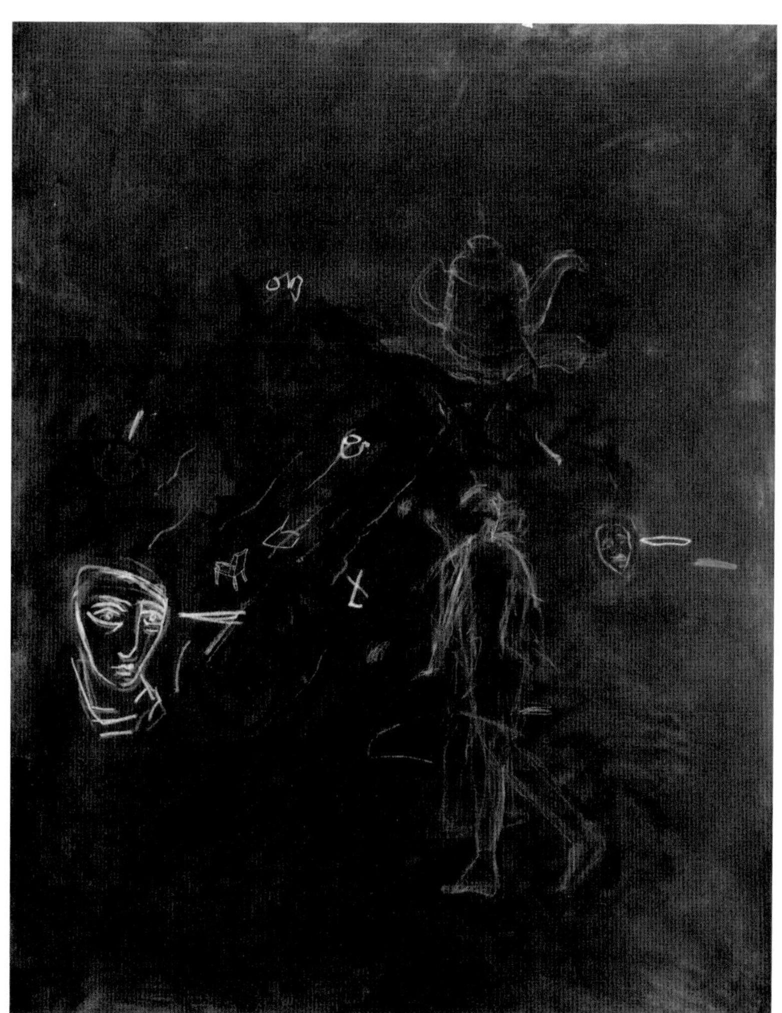

A Slight Ache, 1983
Oil and pencil on canvas
59¾ x 47½"
Collection Rotan Mosle Inc., Division of
Paine-Webber Group

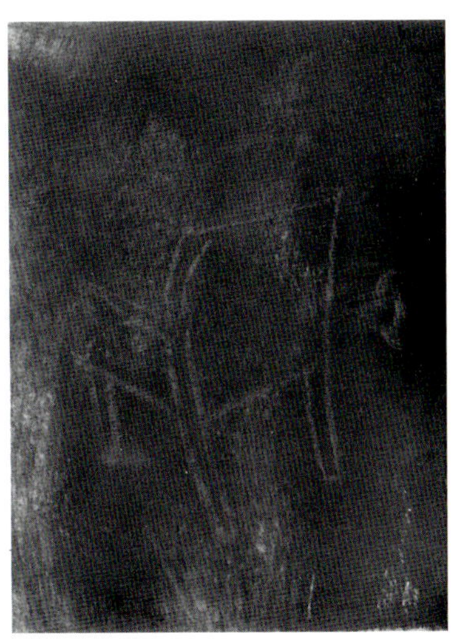

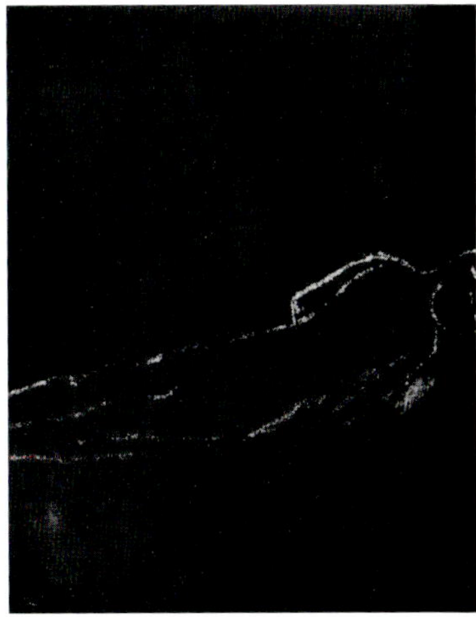

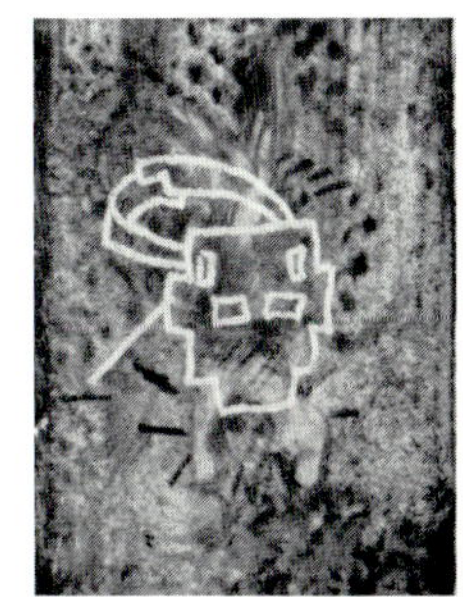

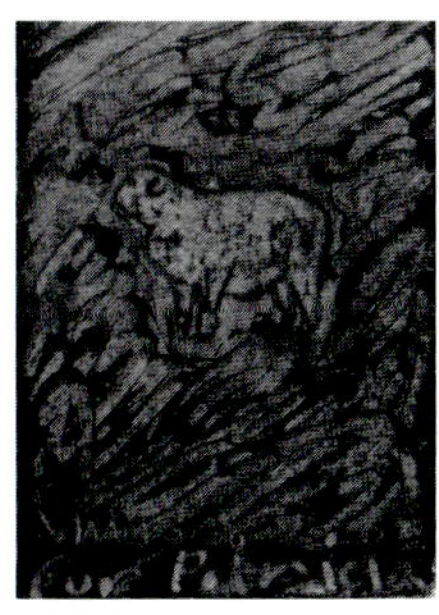

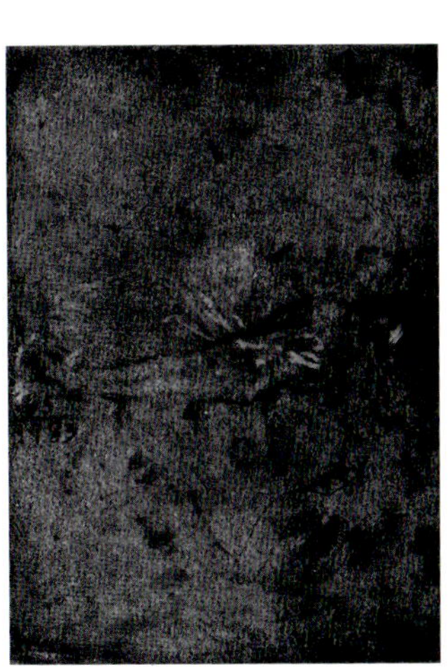

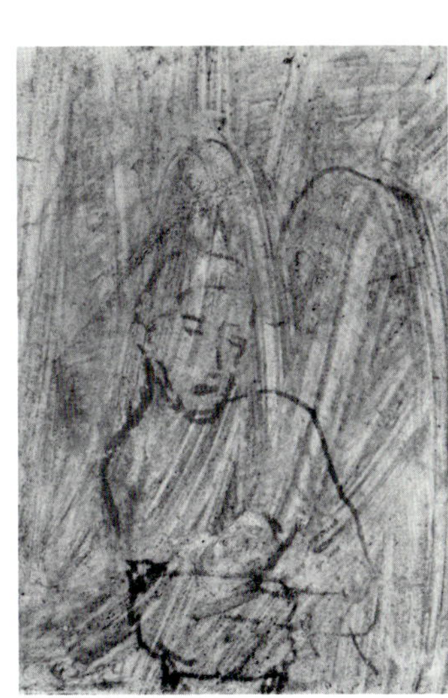

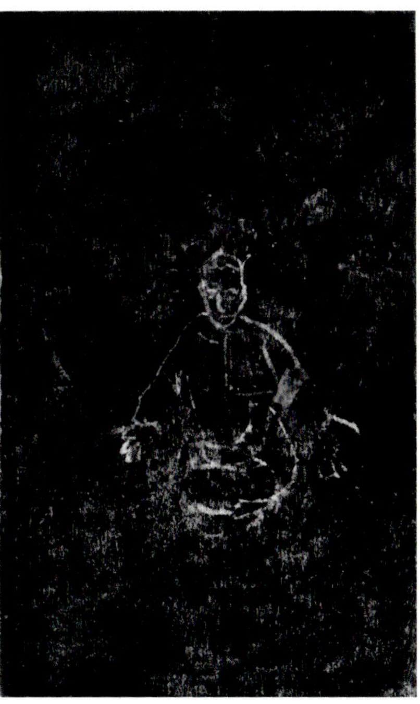

Untitled, 1983
Oil and pencil on paper
4½ x 3½"
Collection Kathy and Karl Kilian, Houston

Untitled, 1983
Oil and pencil on paper
4¾ x 3½"
Private collection

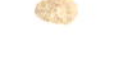

Untitled, 1983
Oil and pencil on paper
4¼ x 3⅛"
Collection Paul Stack, Austin

Untitled, 1985
Oil and pencil on paper
3¼ x 2¼"
Collection Mr. and Mrs. Alexander D. Stuart,
Houston

Untitled (for Derek and for Patricia),
1982
Mixed media on paper
Two panels, each 2¼ x 1⅝"
Collection Derek Boshier and Patricia
Gonzalez, Houston

Untitled, 1985
Mixed media on paper
5½ x 3½"
Collection William Steen, Houston

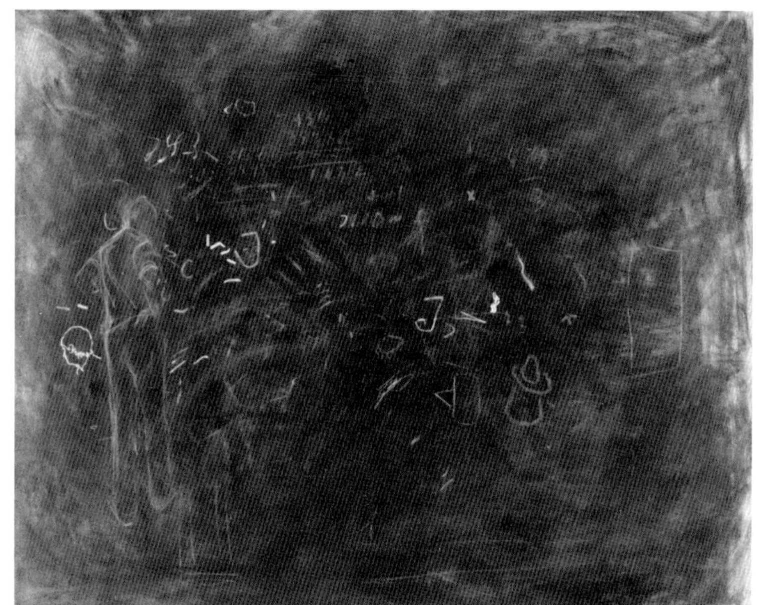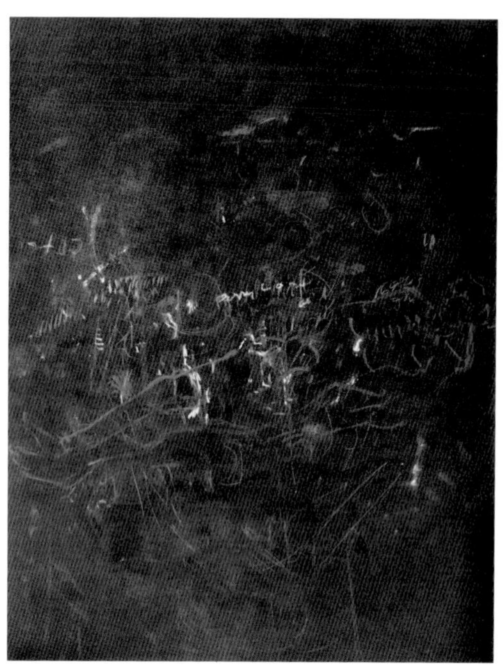

Untitled, 1984
Oil on canvas
47⅞ x 59⅝"
Collection The Museum of Fine Arts, Houston
Museum purchase with funds provided by
Texas Eastern Corporation

Untitled, 1985
Oil on canvas
52 x 40"
Courtesy Janie C. Lee Gallery, Houston and
New York, and Moody Gallery, Houston

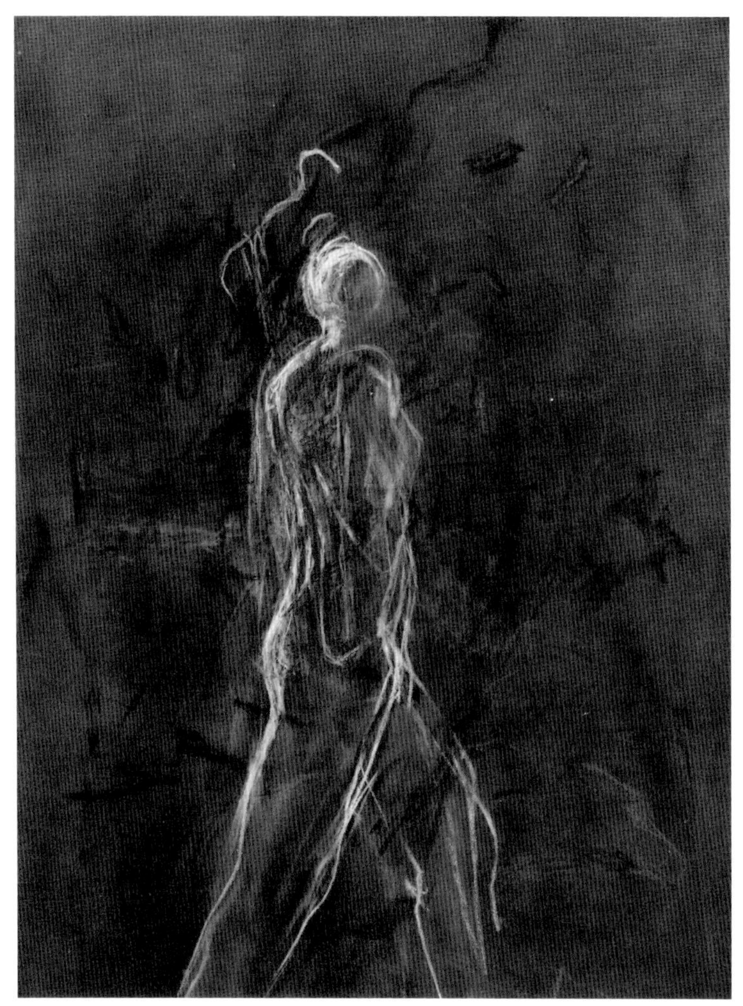

Untitled, 1984
Oil and mixed media on canvas
50 x 38¼"
Collection Mrs. Hugo V. Neuhaus, Jr., Houston

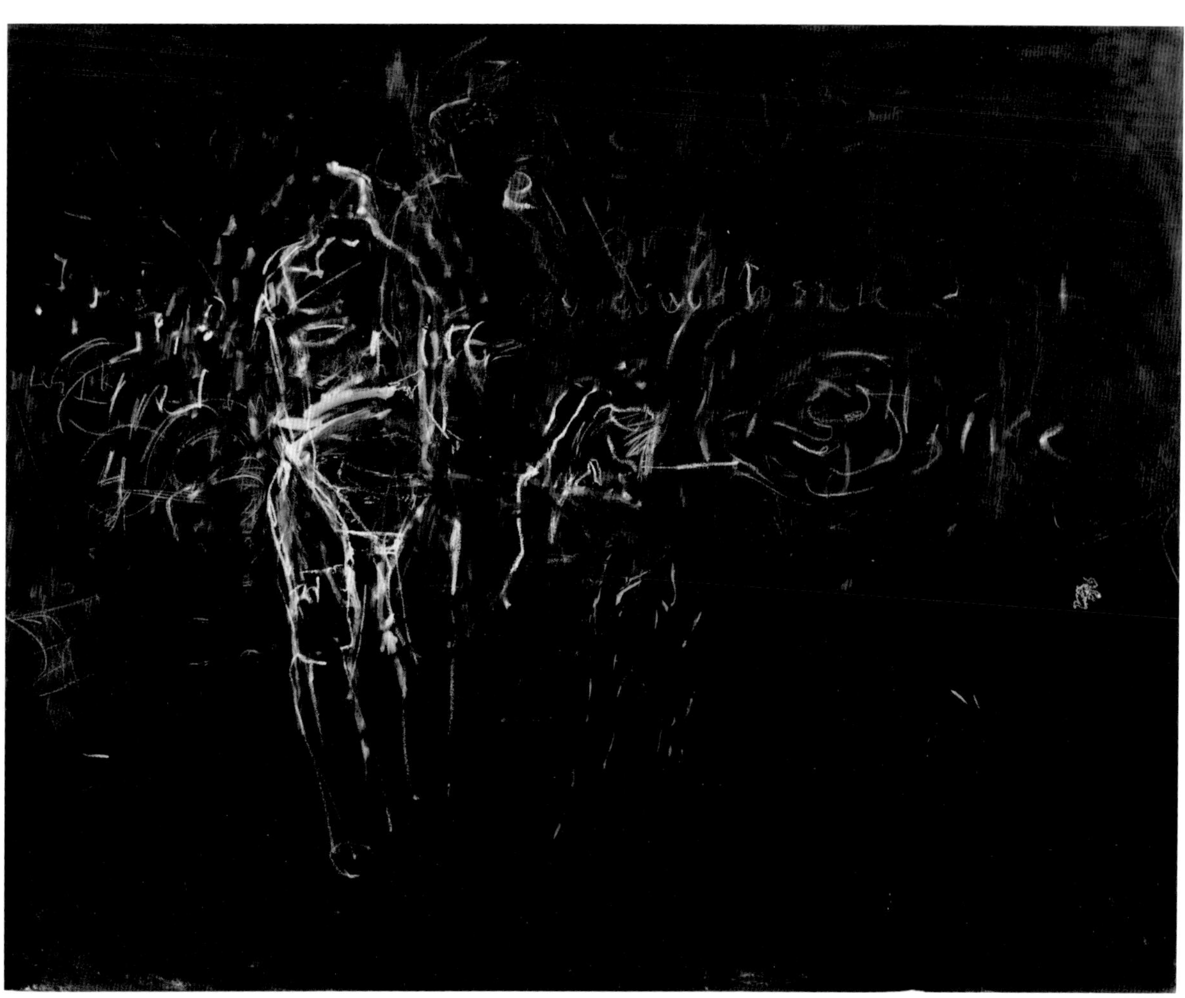

Lesson 4 (for Al), 1985
Oil on canvas
47¾ x 60"
Collection Al Souza, San Diego

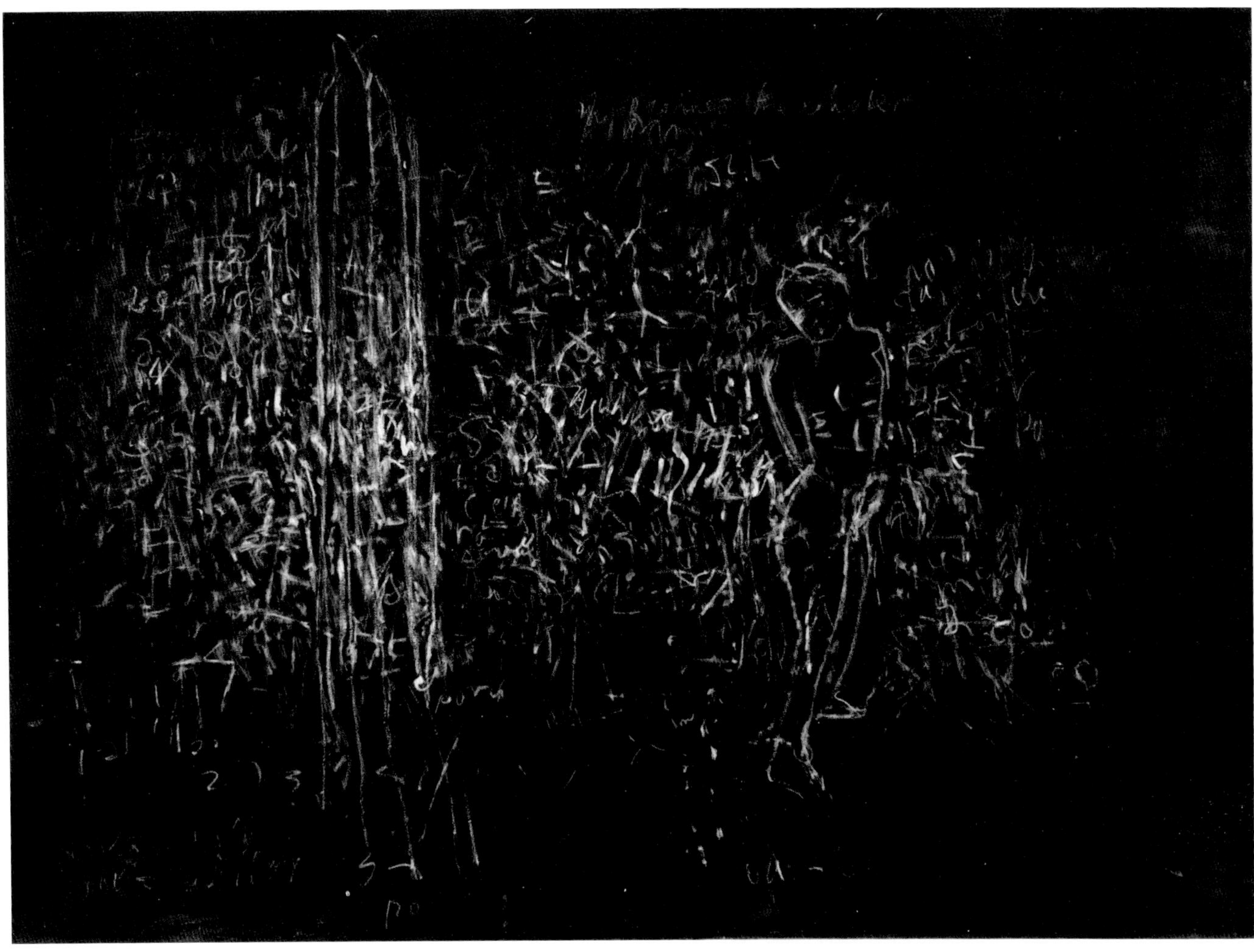

The Last Lesson, 1985
Oil on canvas
48 x 65½"
Courtesy Janie C. Lee Gallery, Houston and
New York, and Moody Gallery, Houston

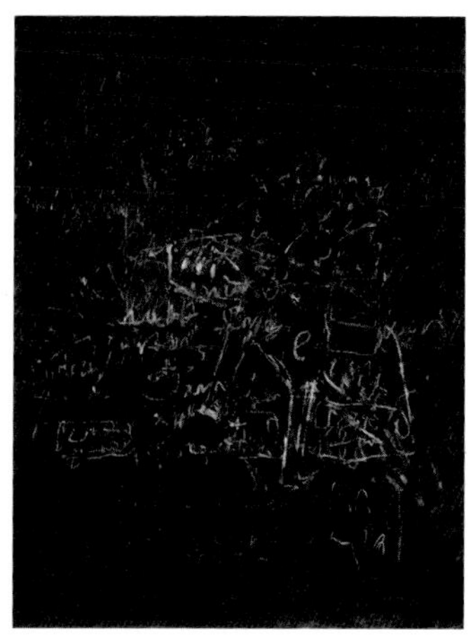

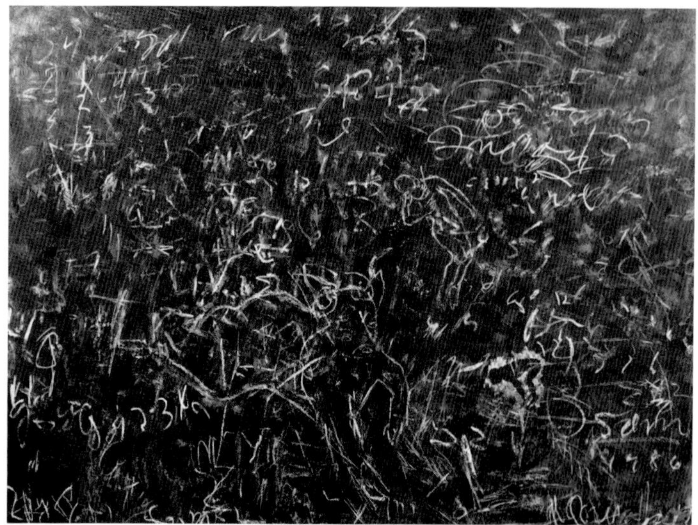

Untitled (for Tim), 1985
Oil on paper
27 x 20¾"
Collection William F. Stern, Houston

A Girl Still, 1986
Oil paint and oil stick on paper
30 x 40"
Courtesy Janie C. Lee Gallery, Houston and
New York

Hedge, 1986
Oil on paper
40 x 30"
Collection Dr. and Mrs. Stuart Linde, Houston

T(oa)d, 1986
Mixed media on paper
21 x 27"
Courtesy David Beitzel Gallery, New York

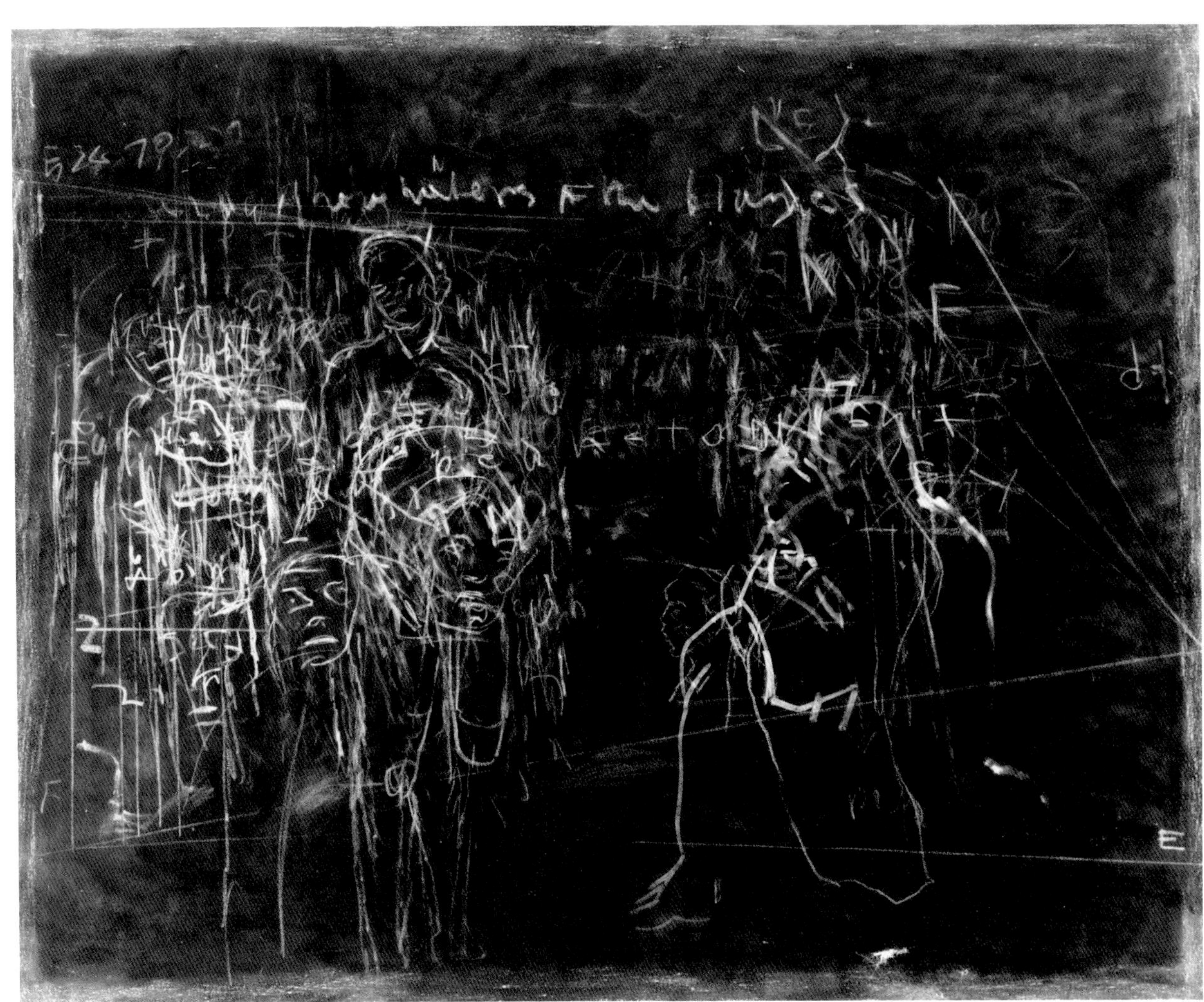

Untitled, 1985
Oil on canvas
48 x 60"
Courtesy Janie C. Lee Gallery, Houston and
New York, and Moody Gallery, Houston

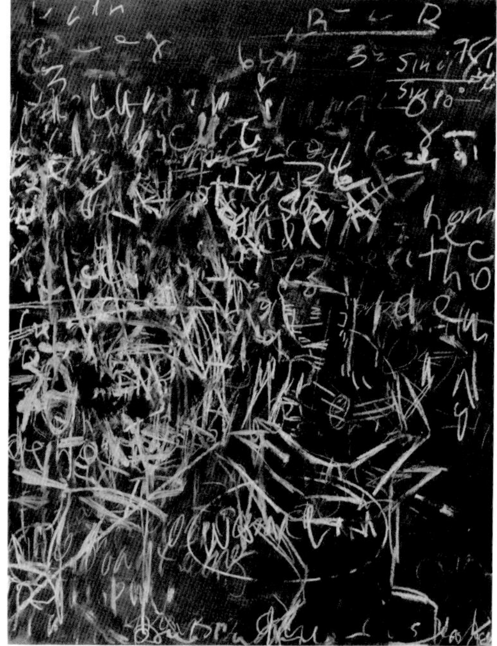

Untitled, 1987
Mixed media on paper
21 x 27"
Collection The Prudential Insurance Company
of America, New York

Untitled, 1987
Mixed media on paper
12½ x 14¾"
Anonymous loan

Untitled, 1986
Mixed media on paper
21¼ x 27½"
Private collection, Texas

Untitled, 1986
Mixed media on paper
13 x 9"
Collection Mr. and Mrs. E. Rudge Allen,
Houston

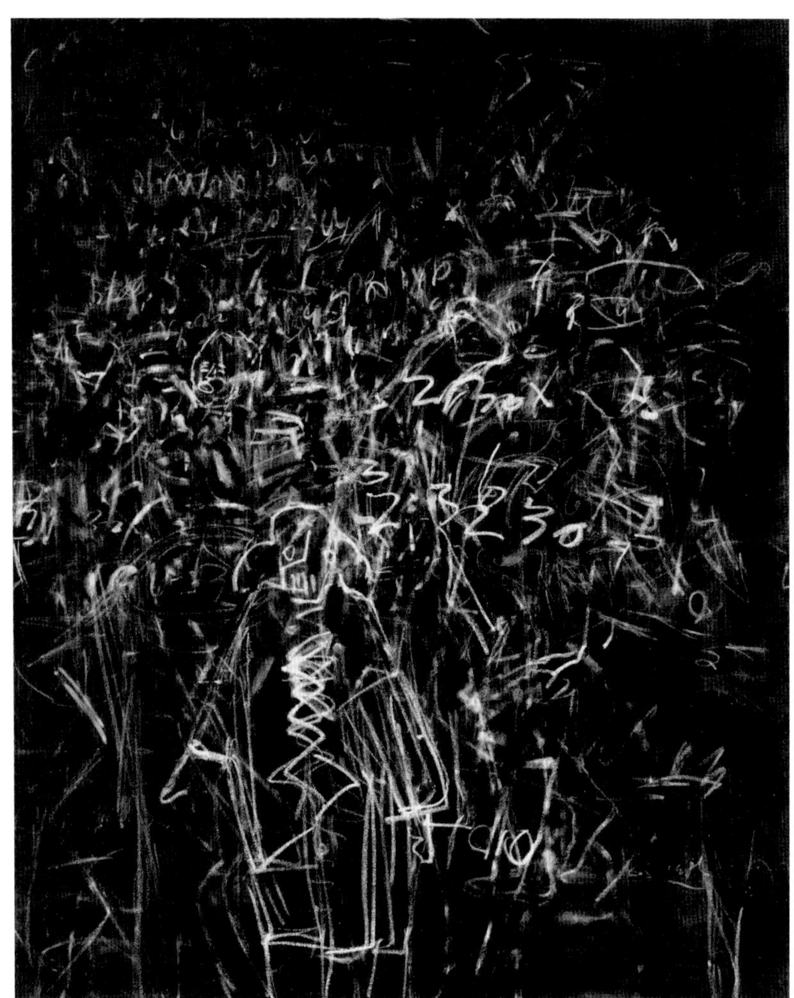

Untitled (Audit), 1986
Oil on canvas
48 x 39"
Courtesy David Beitzel Gallery, New York, and
Moody Gallery, Houston

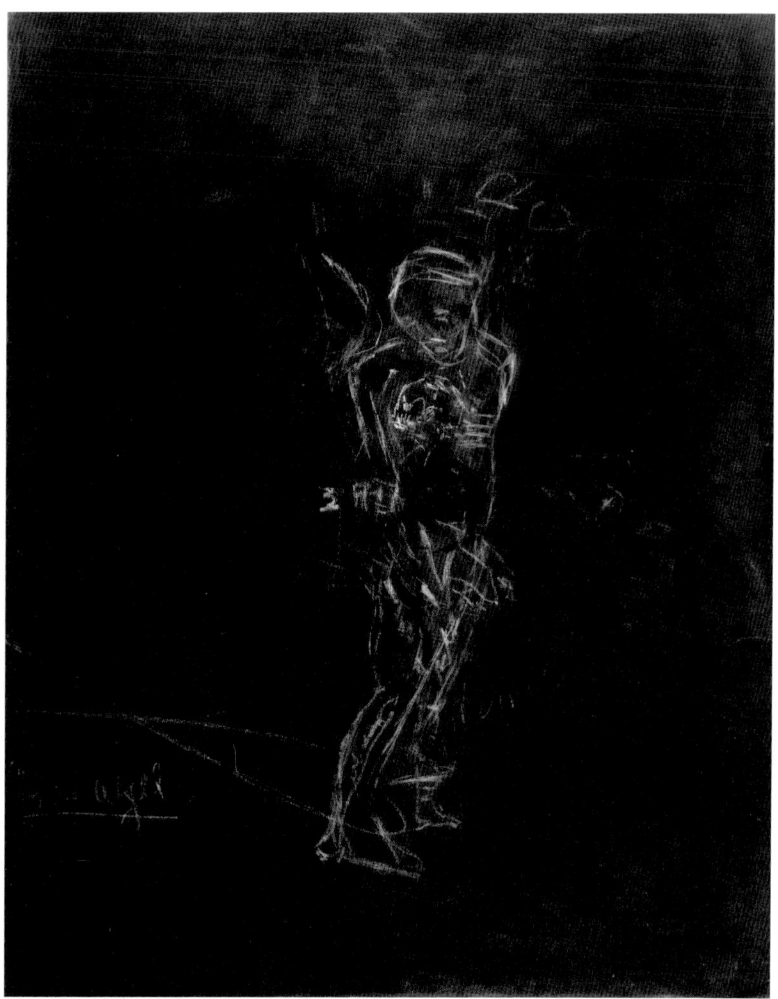

Belayed, 1987
Oil on canvas
60 x 48"
Courtesy David Beitzel Gallery, New York, and
Moody Gallery, Houston

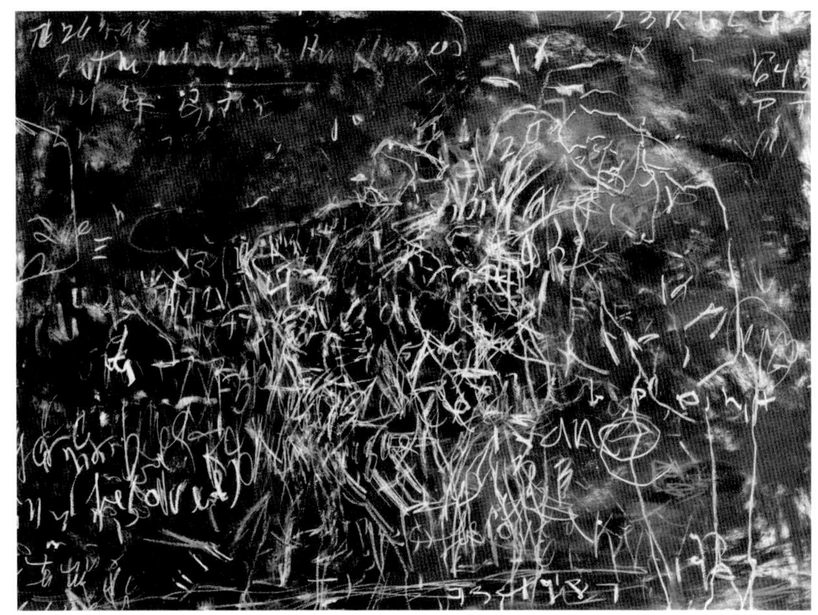

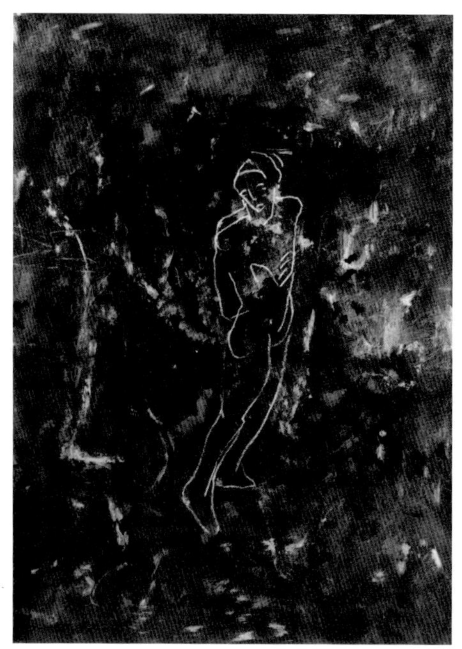

Beloved/Boo, Baby, 1987
Mixed media on paper
28 x 37⅞"
Collection Balene McCormick, Houston

Untitled, 1987
Mixed media on paper
27⅞ x 20"
Courtesy Janie C. Lee Gallery, Houston and
New York

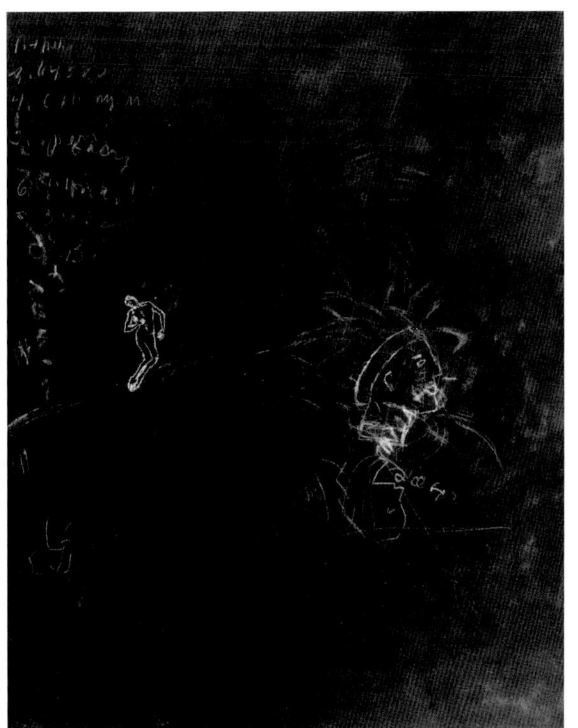

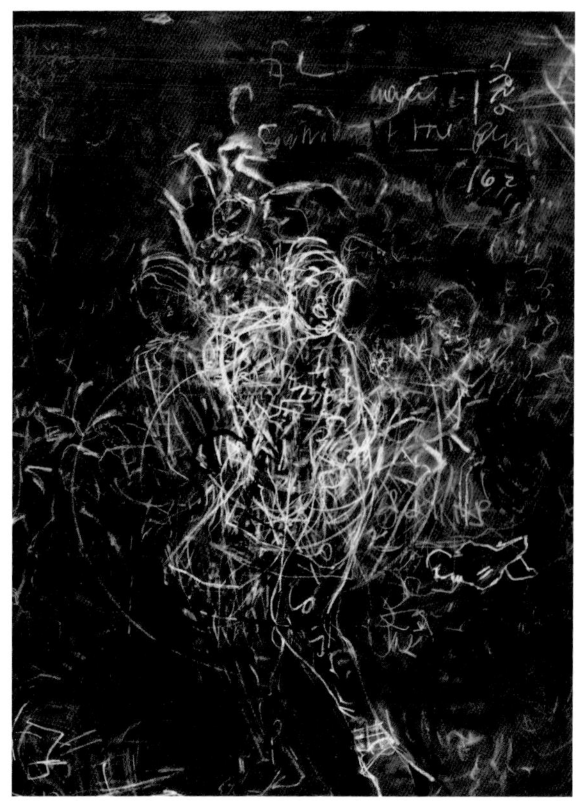

Untitled (The Indian), 1987
Oil on canvas
60 x 48"
Courtesy David Beitzel Gallery, New York, and
Moody Gallery, Houston

Other Graces, 1987
Oil on canvas
65¾ x 48"
Courtesy David Beitzel Gallery, New York, and
Moody Gallery, Houston

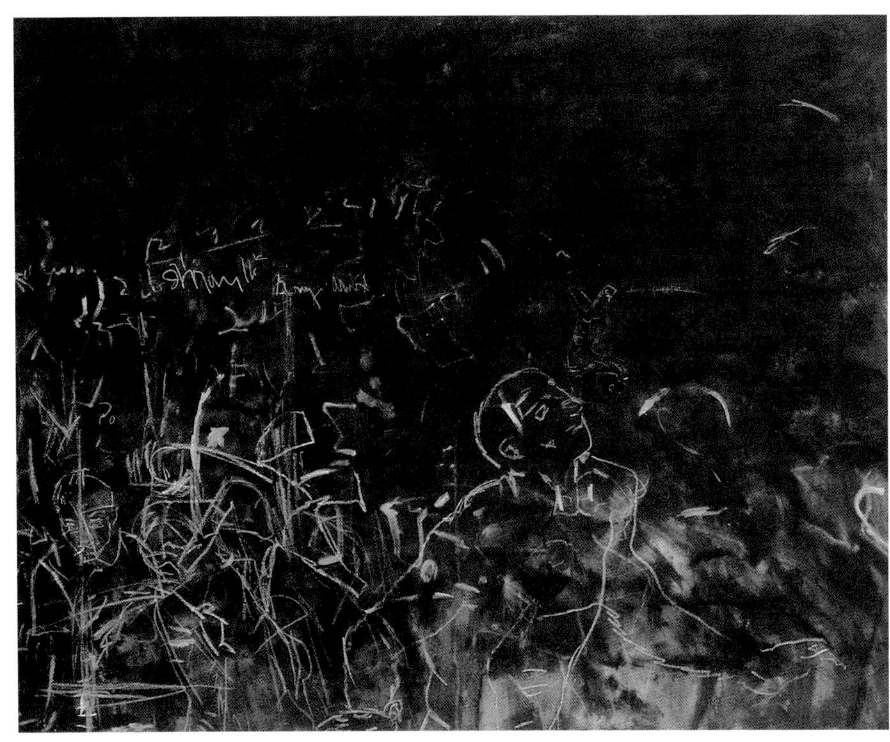

The Revisionist, 1987-88
Oil on canvas
60 x 76"
Collection Linda Cipriani and Gary Horning,
Houston

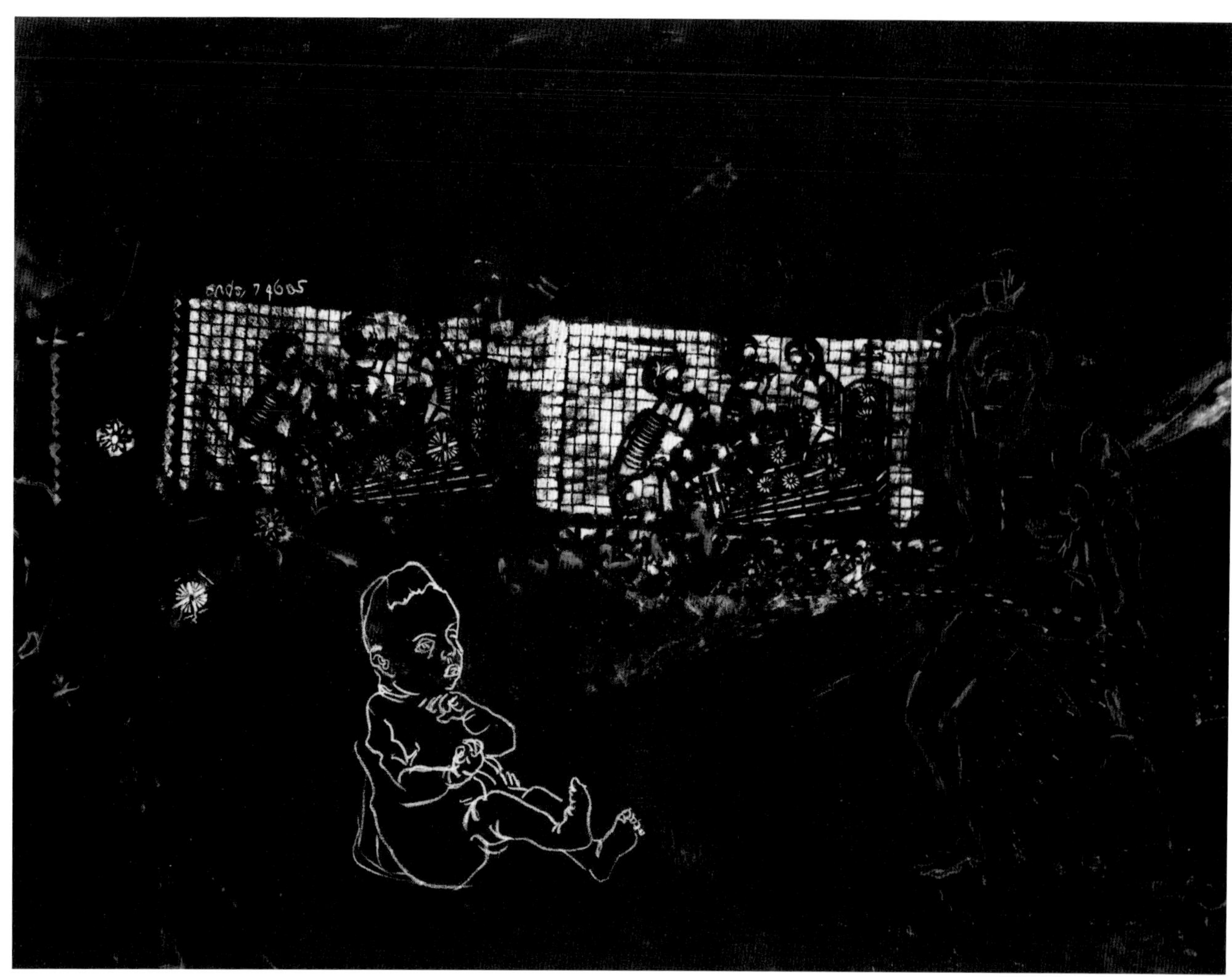

Christmas Picture, 1987-88
Oil on canvas
64 x 84"
Courtesy David Beitzel Gallery, New York, and
Moody Gallery, Houston

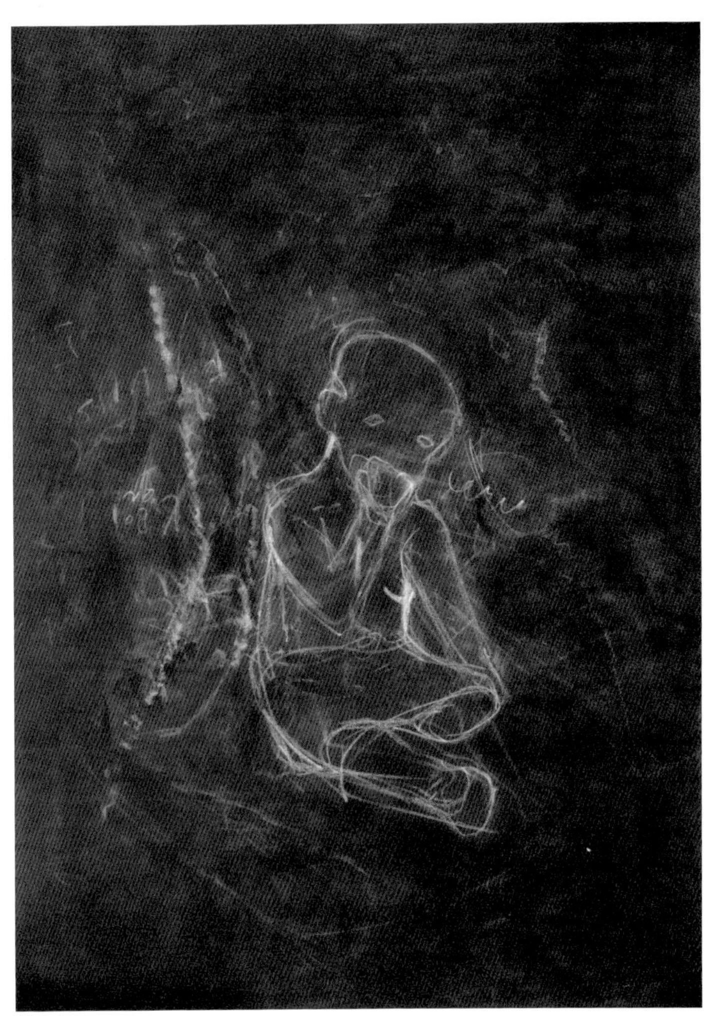

Untitled, 1988
Oil on canvas
66 x 48"
The Menil Collection, Houston

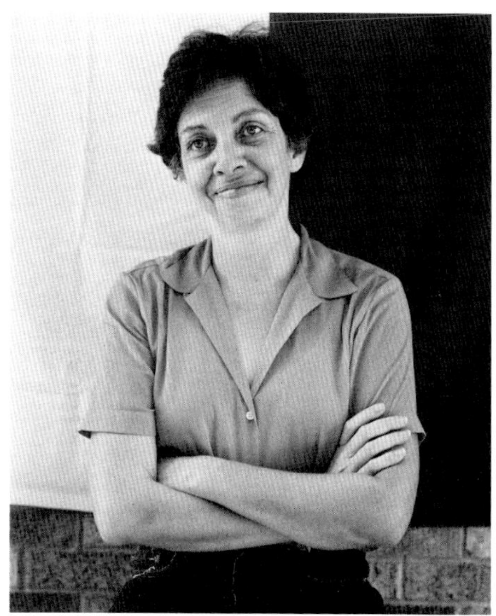

Stack, Houston, 1981

Chronology

Only exhibitions marking significant points in the artist's career are noted in this chronology. See page 82 for a complete exhibition history and bibliography.

1941   Born Kathleen Gael Zender in Chicago.

1959-63   Studies journalism and art at the University of Illinois, Champaign.

1963   Marries.

1964   Paul Michael Stack is born in Chicago. Moves to Gainesville, Florida.

1966   Moves to DeKalb, Illinois.

1967   Moves to Normal, Illinois. Timothy William Stack is born.

1968   Is divorced. Moves with children to Los Angeles. Works as a secretary at the University of Southern California, Los Angeles. Returns to Normal; works at the Chamber of Commerce to earn money to return to college.

1969-70   Studies art at the University of Illinois, Champaign. Receives Bachelor of Fine Arts degree. Begins exhibiting regionally.

1970-72   Pursues graduate studies at Southern Illinois University, Carbondale. Receives Master of Fine Arts degree.

1972-73   Teaches painting at the University of Wisconsin, La Crosse.

1973-74   Moves to Houston. Is employed by the Contemporary Arts Museum as instructor in the *Art After School* program. Teaches art at the High School for the Performing and Visual Arts. In January, 1974, accepts part-time teaching position in the Department of Art, University of Houston. First one-person exhibition, Graphics Gallery, San Francisco.

1975   First one-person exhibition at Meredith Long & Company, Houston.
        Is appointed to the faculty at the University of Houston with the
        rank of assistant professor.

1977   One-person museum exhibition, Art Museum of South Texas,
        Corpus Christi.

1979   Begins painting on canvas. First exhibition of paintings, Meredith
        Long & Company, Houston.

1980   Is promoted to associate professor, University of Houston. Travels
        to Europe for the first time, spends summer in Italy studying
        Italian primitive painting. Begins "blackboard" paintings.

1981   Is included in *19 Artists–Emergent Americans: 1981 Exxon
        National Exhibition* at the Solomon R. Guggenheim Museum, New
        York and *Four Painters: Jones, Smith, Stack, Utterback* at the
        Contemporary Arts Museum, Houston. Travels to England, Wales
        and Austria.

1982   Is awarded National Endowment for the Arts Individual Artist
        Fellowship. Travels to the Netherlands, Belgium and Luxembourg.

1983   First one-person exhibition at Janie C. Lee Gallery, Houston.

1984   Is appointed member, Municipal Arts Commission, City of
        Houston, by Mayor Kathryn J. Whitmire.

1985   Receives Creative Artist Award, Cultural Arts Council of Houston.
        One-person exhibition, Hadler/Rodriguez Galleries, New York.
        Is promoted to full professor. Travels to London, Paris and Spain.
        Begins "lesson" paintings.

1986   Receives Tiffany Foundation Fellowship. Spends spring semester
        teaching in London through the University of Houston's London
        Program. Travels to Spain and Italy.

1987   Is included in *Emerging Artists 1978–1986: Selections from the
        Exxon Series* at the Solomon R. Guggenheim Museum, New York.

1988   First one-person exhibition at David Beitzel Gallery, New York. Is
        elected to the Board of Trustees, Contemporary Arts Museum.

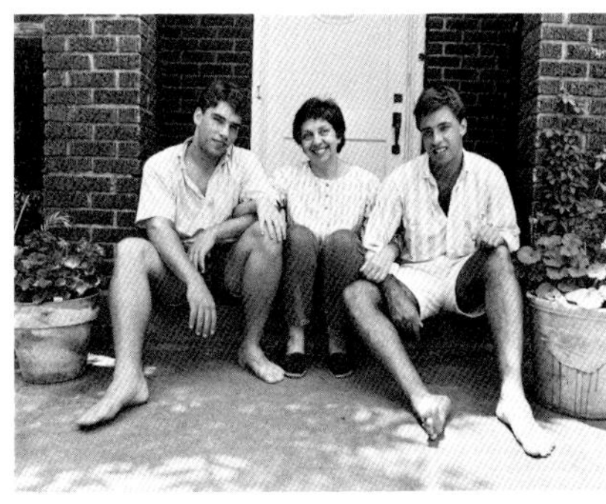

Timothy, Gael, and Paul Stack, Houston, 1986

**One-Artist
Exhibitions and Reviews**

1974
Graphics Gallery, San Francisco.
Jan. 2-Feb. 2.

Albright, Thomas. "Unusual Art in San Francisco." *San Francisco Chronicle*, Jan. 7, 1974, p. 41.

Marlowe, John. "In San Francisco." *Westart*, Jan. 11, 1974, p. 2.

1975
Small Store Gallery, Houston. Mar. 12-31.

Moser, Charlotte. "Three Current Shows Give a Good Sampling of Locally Produced Art." *Houston Chronicle*, Mar. 16, 1975, sec. "Zest," p. 38.

Meredith Long & Company, Houston. July 25-Aug. 6.

Moser, Charlotte. "Bigger Art Has Never Meant Better Art." *Houston Chronicle*, Aug. 3, 1975, sec. "Zest," p. 12.

1976
Meredith Long & Company, Houston. June 17-26.

Holmes, Ann. "Stanczak-Albers Student, but Work Reflects own Ideas." *Houston Chronicle,* June 27, 1976, sec. "Zest," p. 2.

1977
Meredith Long & Company, Houston. Apr. 28-May 28.

Moser, Charlotte. "Galleries Are Moving, Art Isn't." *Houston Chronicle*, May 7, 1977, sec. 2, p. 8.

Art Museum of South Texas, Corpus Christi. Nov. 3-Dec. 18.

1978
Meredith Long & Company, Houston. Aug. 2-Sept. 2.

1979
Meredith Long & Company, Houston. Apr. 15-May 13.

1980
Meredith Long & Company, Houston. Mar. 13-Apr. 18.

Tennant, Donna. "Reviews." *Houston Chronicle*, Apr. 3, 1980, sec. 5, p. 14.

1981
Meredith Long & Company, Houston. June 23-July.

Johnson, Patricia C. "Viewer Gets Pleasure of Attempting to Unravel Mysteries of 'Witches.'" *Houston Chronicle*, June 27, 1981, sec. 3, p. 5.

1983
Janie C. Lee Gallery, Houston.

Johnson, Patricia C. "Reviews." *Houston Chronicle*, Oct. 2, 1983, sec. "Zest," p. 16.

Kalil, Susie. "Houston Galleries Following Trend Toward Regional Art." *The Houston Post*, Oct. 2, 1983, sec. F, p. 8.

1985
Hadler/Rodriguez Galleries, New York. Mar. 9-30.

Brown-Lupton Gallery, Texas Christian University, Fort Worth. Oct. 22-Nov. 1.

Janie C. Lee Gallery, Houston. Dec. 5, 1985-Jan. 10, 1986.

Bloom, Suzanne and Ed Hill. "Reviews: Houston: Gael Stack." *Artforum*, vol. 24, no. 7, Mar. 1986, p. 125.

Johnson, Patricia C. "Stack Fights Battles of Revelation." *Houston Chronicle*, Dec. 14, 1985, sec. 6, p. 1.

McBride, Elizabeth. "Three Houston Painters." *Houston Art Scene*, vol. 7, no. 12, Spring 1986, p. 7.

Tennant, Donna. "Reviews: Houston Letter." *Artspace*, vol. 10, no. 2, Spring 1986, pp. 53-54.

1987
Janie C. Lee Gallery, Houston. *Gael Stack: New Drawings*, Jan. 29-Feb.

Chadwick, Susan. "Gael Stack at Janie C. Lee Gallery." *The Houston Post*, Feb. 8, 1987, sec. F, p. 8.

Johnson, Patricia C. "Touring the Galleries." *Houston Chronicle*, Feb. 8, 1987, sec. "Zest," p. 18.

1988
David Beitzel Gallery, New York. Feb. 4-27.

Group Exhibitions and Reviews

1970
Evansville Museum of Arts and Science, Indiana. *1970 Mid-States Art Exhibition*, Nov. 8-Dec. 6. Cat.

1971
Brooks Memorial Art Gallery, Memphis, Tennessee. *16th Annual Mid-South Exhibition*, Feb. 26-Mar. 28. Cat.

Evansville Museum of Arts and Science, Indiana. *1971 Mid-States Art Exhibition*, Nov. 7-Dec. 5. Cat.

Society of the Four Arts, Palm Beach, Florida. *33rd Annual Exhibition of Contemporary American Paintings*, Dec. 4-26. Cat.

DeMarcellus, Juliette. "Art Show Is Bright and Imaginative." *Palm Beach Times*, Dec. 3, 1971, sec. B, p. 1.

1972
Brooks Memorial Art Gallery, Memphis, Tennessee. *17th Annual Mid-South Exhibition*, Mar.

Sheldon Swope Art Gallery, Terre Haute, Indiana. *28th Annual Wabash Valley Exhibition*, Mar. 5-Apr. 9. Cat.

Downey Museum of Art, California. *15th Annual Art Unlimited*, June 18-July 23.

University of Wisconsin, Stevens Point. *Wisconsin '72*, Oct.-Nov.

University of Wisconsin, Platteville. *Tri-State Exhibition*, Nov. 1-30. Cat.

1973
Anoka-Ramsey State Junior College, Coon Rapids, Minnesota. *Images '73*, Mar. 30-Apr. 27. Cat.

Ball State University, Muncie, Indiana. *19th Drawing and Small Sculpture Show*, May-June. Cat.

1974
Sarah Campbell Blaffer Gallery, University of Houston. *1974 Houston Area Exhibition*, Feb. 2-Mar. 1. Cat.

"Juried Exhibition at Blaffer," *The Houston Post*, Feb. 3, 1974, sec. "Spotlight," p. 32.

Museum of Art, University of Oklahoma, Norman. *16th Annual National Exhibition of Prints and Drawings*, Apr. 7-May 5.

University of St. Thomas, Houston. *New Girls in Town: Suzanne Manns, Gael Stack, Salle Werner*, Apr. 8-Apr. 24.

Del Mar College, Corpus Christi, Texas. *8th Annual National Drawing and Small Sculpture Show.* May 5-31.

One Allen Center, Houston. *Some Other Artists*, May 6-May 30.

Moser, Charlotte. "By Women, for Women." *The Houston Post*, May 12, 1974, sec. "Spotlight," p. 8.

1975
Sarah Campbell Blaffer Gallery, University of Houston. *1975 Houston Area Exhibition*, June 1-July 20. Cat.

Sarah Campbell Blaffer Gallery, University of Houston. *1975 Art Faculty Exhibition*, Dec. 2-18.

Meredith Long & Company, Houston.

1976
University of St. Thomas, Houston. *Valentine Show*, Feb.

The Museum of Fine Arts, Houston. *New Acquisitions: Works on Paper*, Sept. 14-Nov. 14.

Arkansas Arts Center, Little Rock. *19th Annual Delta Exhibition*, Oct. 15-Nov. 14.

Tomlinson Gallery, Albuquerque, New Mexico. *Paper*, Dec. 5-Jan. 31. Cat.

Peterson, William. "Reviews: The Paper Show." *Artspace*, vol. 1, no. 3, Spring 1977, pp. 46-47.

Exhibition Center, Kuwait. *Seven American Artists*.

1977
Moody Gallery, Houston. *Houston Prints*, organized by Little Egypt Enterprises, June 26-July 16.

Alley Theater, Houston. *Art: Women: Houston*, Oct. 14-Nov. 27. Cat.

Crossley, Mimi. "Reviews: Women in Art." *The Houston Post*, Oct. 27, 1977, sec. B, p. 12.

1978
Sarah Campbell Blaffer Gallery, University of Houston. *1978 Art Faculty Exhibition*, Mar. 4-Apr. 9.

N.A.M.E. Gallery, Chicago. *7 x 9*, June 16-July 8.

Southern Illinois University, Carbondale.

1979
Contemporary Arts Museum, Houston. *Fire!*, Feb. 16-Apr. 15. Cat.

Alley Theater, Houston. *Doors: Houston Artists*, Mar. 17-25. Cat. Traveled to The Art Center, Waco, Texas.

Crossley, Mimi. "Review: Doors by 54 Houston Artists." *The Houston Post*, Mar. 23, 1979, sec. E, p. 11.

Lawndale Art Annex, University of Houston. *Pow-Wow Miniature Show*, Aug. 31-Sept. 20.

Galveston Arts Center, Texas. *Prints '79*, Nov. 25-Dec. 12.

Instituto Allende, San Miguel de Allende, Guanajuato, Mexico. *Works on Paper.*

1980
Contemporary Arts Center, New Orleans. *Texas Invitational*, May 2-23.

Sarah Campbell Blaffer Gallery, University of Houston. *1980 Houston Area Exhibition*, June 7-July 27. Cat.

Tennant, Donna. "Cool, Calm, Collected." *Houston Chronicle*, June 15, 1980, sec. AA, p. 17.

1981
Solomon R. Guggenheim Museum, New York. *19 Artists–Emergent Americans: 1981 Exxon National Exhibition*, Jan. 30-Apr. 5. Cat., text by Thomas M. Messer and Peter Frank.

Larson, Kay. "The Great American Talent Hunt." *New York Magazine*, vol. 14, no. 8, Feb. 23, 1981, pp. 51-54.

Rickey, Carrie. "Curatorial Conceptions, the Guggenheim: Singular Pluralism." *Artforum*, vol. 19, no. 8, Apr. 1981, pp. 58-60.

Roberts, A. H. "Gael Stack at Guggenheim." *Houston Art Scene*, vol. 2, no. 6, May/June 1981, p. 4.

Schjeldahl, Peter. "Stock Options." *The Village Voice*, Feb. 18-24, 1981, p. 73.

Roberto Molina Gallery, Houston. *Works on Paper,* Mar. 24-Apr. 7.

Brown-Lupton Gallery, Texas Christian University, Fort Worth. *Works by Women,* Sept. 21-Oct. 9. Traveled regionally through Jan. 15, 1989.

Sarah Campbell Blaffer Gallery, University of Houston. *1981 Art Faculty Exhibition*, Oct. 10-25.

Contemporary Arts Museum, Houston. *Four Painters: Jones, Smith, Stack, Utterback*, Oct. 10-Nov. 29. Cat., text by Linda L. Cathcart and Marti Mayo.

Crossley, Mimi. "Review: Four Poetic Painters." *The Houston Post*, Oct. 18, 1981, sec. AA, p. 12.

Johnson, Patricia C. "Painting From the Inside." *Houston Chronicle*, Oct. 18, 1981, sec. "Zest," p. 18.

Kalil, Susie. "Four Painters at the Contemporary Arts Museum." *Art in America*, vol. 70, no. 4, Apr. 1982, pp. 144-145.

Patrick Gallery, Austin, Texas. *Mythmakers and Storytellers*, Oct. 27-Nov. 21.

Optima Studios, New Orleans. *Works on Paper.*

1982
Contemporary Arts Museum, Houston. *Texas on Paper,* Feb. 5-Mar 14. Cat., text by Cheryl A. Brutvan and Linda L. Cathcart. Traveled.

Stavanger Kunstforening, Norway. *Art from Houston in Norway: 1982*, June 3-28. Cat., text by David Brauer and Robin Cronin.

Galerie Simone Stern, New Orleans. Sept. 11-30.

Green, Roger. "Vision: The World of Art." *The Times-Picayune*, Sept. 26, 1982, sec. 3, pp. 6-7.

The Museum of Fine Arts, Houston. *New Accessions: Texas Artists*, Oct. 4-Nov.

Meredith Long & Company, Houston. *Americans on Paper.*

1983
New Orleans Museum of Art. *1983 New Orleans Triennial*. Apr. 8-May 22. Cat., text by William A. Fagaly and Linda L. Cathcart.

Vetrocq, Marcia E. "1983 Triennial at the New Orleans Museum of Art." *Art in America*, vol. 71, no. 9, Oct. 1983, pp. 191-193.

Salzburger Kunstverein, Austria. *New Art from a New City: Houston*, June 8-July 3. Cat., text by William A. Camfield. Traveled to Galerie an der Stadtmauer, Villach, Austria.

Contemporary Arts Museum, Houston. *Southern Fictions*, Aug. 2-Sept. 4. Cat., text by William A. Fagaly and Monroe K. Spears.

Bassin, Joan. "Art of the South." *Austin American-Statesman*, Aug. 28, 1983, p. 37.

Johnson, Patricia C. "The Tangible Enigma of the South." *Houston Chronicle,* Aug. 7, 1983, "Zest," p. 13.

Kalil, Susie. "Art: 'Southern Fictions.'" *The Houston Post*, Aug. 7, 1983, sec. F, p. 1.

Sarah Campbell Blaffer Gallery, University of Houston, *1983 Art Faculty Exhibition*, Oct. 14-30.

Midtown Art Center, *A Salute to Houston Artists*, Oct. 29-Nov.

1984
Two Houston Center. *1984 Show,* organized by the Assistance League of Houston, Mar. 6-24. Cat., text by Ron Gleason.

Hadler/Rodriguez Galleries, New York. *Works on Paper,* Mar. 9-30.

Janie C. Lee Gallery, Houston. *Four Texas Painters: John Alexander, Sam Gummelt, Philip Renteria, Gael Stack.* May.

Diverse Works, Houston. *Texas Artists in Houston Corporate Collections*, May 3-June 11.

San Antonio Art Institute. *Word Images*, Sept. 27-Nov. 8

Boothe-Meredith, Sally. "Words, Welds by Texas Artists." *The Sunday Express-News*, Oct. 14, 1984, sec. B, p. 12.

Solon, Marcia Goren. "Written Word Joins Unwritten." *San Antonio Light*, Oct. 7, 1984, sec. H, p. 1.

College of the Mainland Art Gallery, Texas City. *Houston Figurative Art*, Nov. 4-Dec. 6. Cat.

1985
Drawing Room Gallery, Houston. *Fresh Roots: First Marks*, Jan. 19-Feb. 8.

Johnson, Patricia C. "Work from Artists' Youth Has Some Surprises." *Houston Chronicle*, Jan. 28, 1985, sec. 4, p. 1.

The Museum of Fine Arts, Houston. *Works on Paper: Eleven Houston Artists*, Jan. 26-Mar. 7. Cat., text by William A. Camfield.

Johnson, Patricia C. "The Houston Connection: MFA Scores Twice with Exhibition." *Houston Chronicle*, Feb. 3, 1985, sec. "Zest," p. 16.

McEvilley, Thomas. "Double Vision in Space City." *Artforum*, vol. 23, no. 8, Apr. 1985, pp. 52-56.

The Museum of Fine Arts, Houston. *Fresh Paint: The Houston School*, Jan. 26-Apr. 7. Cat., text by Barbara Rose and Susie Kalil. Traveled to Institute for Art and Urban Resources, P.S. 1, Long Island City, New York.

Ennis, Michael. "Persistent Vigor." *Texas Monthly*, vol. 13, no. 3, Mar. 1985, pp. 152-157.

Everingham, Carol J. "Comparing, Contrasting Two Different 'Schools' of Art." *The Houston Post*, Feb. 10, 1985, sec. F, p. 3.

Everingham, Carol J. "Fresh Outlook of 'Fresh Paint.'" *The Houston Post*, Feb. 17, 1985, sec. F, p. 1.

Hauser, Reine. "Reviews: Houston: Hometown Bravura." *Artnews*, vol. 84, no. 6, Summer 1985, pp. 103-104.

Holmes, Ann. "Fresh Paint." *Houston Chronicle*, Jan. 20, 1985, sec. "Special Supplement."

Johnson, Patricia C. "Major MFA Show Defines and Celebrates 'Houston School.'" *Houston Chronicle*, Jan. 26, 1985, sec. 4, p. 1.

Kutner, Janet. "Wrong Brush Strokes." *The Dallas Morning News*, Mar. 27, 1985, sec. F, p. 1.

Larson, Kay. "Art." *New York Magazine*, vol. 18, no. 24, June 17, 1985, pp. 62-64.

McEvilley, Thomas. "Double Vision in Space City." *Artforum*, vol. 23, no. 8, Apr. 1985, pp. 52-56.

Ratcliff, Carter. "On 'Fresh Paint.'" *Artspace*, Summer 1985, pp. 9-11.

Fox Fine Arts Center, The University of Texas at El Paso. *12 Texas Painters*, Feb. 22-Mar. 29. Cat.

San Antonio Art Institute. *Texas Currents*, Sept. 26-Dec. 13. Cat., text by Howard Smagula.

Fisch, Carol. "The State of the Art of the State." *San Antonio Monthly*, vol. 5, no.1, Oct. 1985, pp. 48-51.

Goddard, Dan R. "New 'Currents' in Texas Art." *The Express-News*, Sept. 29, 1985, sec. H, p. 12.

McCombie, Mel. "Vibrant Variety: Talent Flows Throughout 'Texas Currents.'" *Austin American-Statesman*, Nov. 22, 1985, sec. F, p. 3.

Shukalo, Alice. "Art: 'Texas Currents' in San Antonio." *Texas Journal*, vol. 8, no. 1, pp. 42-43.

Lawndale Art and Performance Center, University of Houston. *One Up*, Oct. 25-Nov. 16.

Janie C. Lee Gallery, Houston. *Gallery Artists.*

1986
1600 Smith in Cullen Center, Houston. *Texas Time Machine*, Jan.16-May 15. Cat., text by Joan Seeman Robinson. Traveled to Sheraton Gallery, Dallas.

Kutner, Janet. "Offbeat Views of Texas History." *The Dallas Morning News*, sec. E, p. 1.

Sarah Campbell Blaffer Gallery, University of Houston. *1986 Art Faculty Exhibition*, Jan. 19-Feb. 9.

Janie C. Lee Gallery, Houston. *Paintings, Sculpture, Collages and Drawings*, Mar. 8-Apr.

Butler Gallery, Houston. Sept. 13-Oct 31.

Chadwick, Susan. "Butler's Art Exhibits Show Strength." *The Houston Post*, Oct. 5, 1986, sec. H, p. 4.

Glassell School of Art, The Museum of Fine Arts, Houston. *Houston Drawing*, Sept. 30-Oct. 23.

Diverse Works, Houston. *Prisoners of Conscience: A Collaboration* with *Amnesty International*, Nov. 8-23. Cat.

Galerie Dario Boccara, Paris. *Cinq x Cinq: Houston, Texas*, Nov. 28-Feb. 7. Cat., text by Gérard-Georges Lemaire.

Bocksch-Juul, Carl. "Le choix des connaisseurs." *Connaissance des arts*, no. 418, Dec. 1986, p. 50.

Edward Totah Gallery, Zurich. *Forum.*

1987
The Museum of Fine Arts, Houston. *Direction and Diversity: Twentieth-Century Art in the Museum Collection*, Jan. 20-25.

Butler Gallery, Houston. Jan. 21-Mar. 21.

Chadwick, Susan. "Gallery's Group Show an Overview." *The Houston Post*, Feb. 8, 1987, sec. F, p. 8.

Art League of Houston. *Selections: 15 Years, Little Egypt Enterprises, 1973-1987*, Apr. 23-May 23.

Solomon R. Guggenheim Museum, New York. *Emerging Artists 1978-1986: Selections from the Exxon Series*, Sept. 4-Oct. 25. Cat., text by Diane Waldman.

Aspen Art Museum, Colorado. *Third Coast Review: A Look at Art in Texas*, Sept. 10-Oct. 25. Cat., text by Annette DiMeo Carlozzi. Traveled regionally through June 12, 1988.

David Beitzel Gallery, New York. *Aaron Fink, Tom Hatch, Chris MacDonald, Gael Stack*, Sept. 18-Oct. 17.

Gallery Nine, University of Illinois, Champaign. *At Conception: Small Drawings for Big Ideas*, Dec. 18-Jan. 30.

1988
College of the Mainland Art Gallery, Texas City. *Selected Texas Women Art Faculty*, Jan. 21-Feb. 25.

Glassell School of Art, The Museum of Fine Arts, Houston. *One + One: Collaborations by Artists and Writers*, Jan. 22-Feb. 25. Cat., text by Donald Barthelme and Janet Landay.

Chadwick, Susan. "Writers, Artists Present United Front Worth Investigating." *The Houston Post*, Jan. 24, 1988, sec. F, p. 12.

Johnson, Patricia C. "Something Old and Something New, Combining Words and Pictures, Too." *Houston Chronicle*, Feb. 14, 1988, sec. "Zest," pp. 18-19.

Robinson, Joan Seeman. "Reviews: Houston: *One + One*, Glassell School of Art." *Artnews*, vol. 87, no. 6, Summer 1988, p. 196.

Southwest Texas State University, San Marcos. *Patricia Gonzalez, Allan Smith, Gael Stack: Recent Paintings*, Feb. 10-25.

The Menil Collection, Richmond Hall, Houston. *Texas Art*, Feb. 10- May 15. Cat., texts by Alison de Lima Greene, Neil Printz and Marilyn Zeitlin.

1600 Smith in Cullen Center, Houston. *Houston '88*, organized by Houston Art Dealers Association, Feb. 11-May 12. Cat.

Janie C. Lee Master Drawings Gallery, New York. *Master Drawings, 1877-1987*, Feb.-Mar.

The Museum of Fine Arts, Houston. *Twentieth-Century Art in the Museum Collection: Direction and Diversity*, May 21-Sept.4.

G.V.G. Gallery, Houston. *Works on Paper*, Aug. 13-Sept. 30.

    Chadwick, Susan. "Group Show of Works on Paper at G.V.G. Gallery." *The Houston Post*, Sept. 4, 1988, sec. F, p. 9.

Moody Gallery, Houston. *Texas Artists*, Sept. 1-20.

    Chadwick, Susan. "Texas Artists, Group Show at Moody Gallery," *The Houston Post*, Sept. 25, 1988, sec. F, p. 4.

Art Museum of Southeast Texas, Beaumont. *Art for the Museum: A Legacy*, Sept. 9-Dec. 4.

1989

The Museum of Fine Arts, Houston. *Diamonds Are Forever*, Jan. 14-Mar.

    Dierker, Larry. "A Celebration of Baseball." *Houston Chronicle,* Jan. 8, 1989, sec. "Texas Magazine," pp. 8-13.

Dallas Museum of Art. *Now/Then/Again*, Jan. 15-June.

Sarah Campbell Blaffer Gallery, University of Houston. *1989 Art Faculty Exhibition*, Jan. 20-Feb. 5.

Bibliography

Books
Carlozzi, Annette DiMeo. *Fifty Texas Artists*. San Francisco: Chronicle Books, 1986.

McBride, Elizabeth, "Psychic Landscapes." In *No Bluebonnets, No Yellow Roses: Essays on Texas Women in the Arts*, edited by Sylvia Moore. New York: Midmarch Press, 1988.

Articles
Smith, Roberta. "Twelve Days of Texas." *Art in America*, vol. 64, no. 4, July/Aug. 1976, pp. 42-48.

Moser, Charlotte. "But on the Other Hand." *Houston City Magazine*, vol. 4, no. 2, Feb. 1980, pp. 54-57.

Schjeldahl, Peter. "Art and Money in the City of Future-Think." *Houston City Magazine*, vol. 4, no. 2, Feb. 1980, pp. 46-54, 97-101.

Glueck, Grace. "How Emerging Artists Really Emerge: Putting the Biennials Together." *Artnews*, vol. 80, no. 5, May 1981, pp. 95-99.

Moser, Charlotte. "Artists the Critics Are Watching." *Artnews*, vol. 80, no. 5, May 1981, pp. 86-87.

"Gael Stack at the Guggenheim." *Houston Chronicle*, May 3, 1981, sec. "Texas Magazine," p. 50.

VanderLee, Jana. "The Houston Image as a New Arts Frontier: Fact, Fiction— or Both?" *Art Voices South*, vol. 4, no. 5, Sept./Oct. 1981, pp. 14-17.

Johnson, Patricia C. "Gael Stack: Artist-teacher Who Doesn't Easily Fit Into a Mold." *Houston Chronicle*, Oct. 4, 1981, sec. "Zest," p. 15.

Kalil, Susie. "Houston Artists: They'd Rather Fight than Switch." *Artnews*, vol. 80, no. 10, Dec. 1981, pp. 103-107.

McKay, Gary. "Four Artists/Four Styles." *Houston Home and Garden*, vol. 8, no. 5, Feb. 1982, pp. 28-34.

VanderLee, Jana. "Gael Stack and Clyde Connell: Hinged on Time." *Artspace*, vol. 7, no. 4, Fall 1983, pp. 23-25.

"The Gihon Art Collection." *Helicon Nine*, no. 11, 1984, pp. 33-41.

Freudenheim, Susan. "Gael Stack: Narrator of Emotions." *Texas Homes*, vol. 8, no. 7, July 1984, pp. 20-24.

Moser, Charlotte. "Regional Revisions: Houston and Chicago." *Art in America*, vol. 73, no. 7, July 1985, pp. 90-99.

Gambrell, Jamey. "Art Capital of the Third Coast." *Art in America*, vol. 75, no. 4, Apr. 1987, pp. 186-203.

"Contemporary Arts Museum Trustees." *Houston Chronicle*, Jan. 26, 1988, sec. 4, p. 3.

McKay, Gary. "Pages From a Diary." *Houston Metropolitan*, vol. 14, no. 11, Aug. 1988, pp. 35-37, 71-74.

Edited by Richard Levy
Designed by Minor Design Group, Inc.
Typesetting by Characters, Inc.
1,500 copies printed by Wetmore & Co.

88

University of Houston

Richard L. Van Horn, *President*

Sarah Campbell Blaffer Gallery Staff

Catherine Angel, *Gallery Attendant*
*Pat Burns, *Preparator*
*Steven Burtch, *Assistant Preparator*
*Monica Chau, *Work-Study Assistant*
Nancy S. Hixon, *Registrar*
Marti Mayo, *Director*
*Marian McEvilley, *Work-Study Assistant*
Rena Minar, *Curatorial Assistant for Education and Public Affairs*
Shiree Schade, *Administrator/Secretary to the Director*
*Elizabeth Ward, *Curatorial Assistant for Exhibitions and Publications*

*Part-time

Board of Regents University of Houston System

Dorothy Alcorn, *Secretary*
Debbie Hanna
C. F. Kendall II
James L. Ketelsen
Kenneth L. Lay, *Chair*
Xavier C. Lemond, *Vice Chair*
Jose E. Molina
R. E. Reamer
Don A. Sanders

Photographic Credits

Gay Block, Houston, p. 81.
Suzanne Bloom, Houston, p. 80.
Cousins Color, New York, p. 53.
D. James Dee, New York, p. 70.
Rick Gardner, Houston, cover and pp. 48, 49, 52, 54, 55, 77.
Vincent Gargotta, Houston, p. 60.
Carmelo Guadagno, New York, p. 34.
Paul Hestor, Houston, p. 79.
Allen Mewbourn, Houston, p. 62.
Zhotograph, Houston, pp. 32, 33, 34, 35, 36, 37, 38, 39, 40, 41, 42, 43, 44, 45, 49, 51, 54, 56, 57, 58, 59, 60, 61, 62, 63, 64, 65, 66, 67, 68, 69, 70, 71, 72, 73, 74, 75, 76, 78.